To: Quincy my
Beautiful Brother in
Christ

Fr: Sister Sunny

In you lives the
awesome power of God's
anointing. You are
His treasure & we love
you in Christ 11/19/2018

"Thus far the Lord has helped us"

"THUS FAR THE LORD HAS HELPED US"

Looking back on
how the Lord has
loved us, led us,
and lavished His
blessings upon us

EDDIE CLOER

RESOURCE □
PUBLICATIONS
2209 S. Benton
Searcy, AR 72143

Copyright © 2002
Eddie Cloer

ISBN: 0-945441-41-X

Scripture taken from the NEW AMERICAN STANDARD BIBLE®, © Copyright The Lockman Foundation 1960, 1962, 1963, 1968, 1971, 1972, 1973, 1975, 1977, 1995. Used by permission. (www.Lockman.org)

DEDICATION

❧

To Our Son
Steve Edward Cloer
A handsome prince
Obedient, conscientious, sensitive,
An excellent scholar of the Scriptures,
A dedicated Christian young man,
Who, I believe, yearns to be all
that Christ wants him to be,
And who has been everything a father and mother
could want their son to be.

"O God, our help in ages past,
Our hope for years to come,
Be Thou our guard while life shall last,
And our eternal home!"

Isaac Watts

Gratitude for our children has caused Susan and me to say in the words of the ancient writer of Psalm 116:12: "What shall I render to the Lord for all His benefits toward me?"

CONTENTS

∾

PREFACE

This book is not an attempt at an autobiography. It is an effort to give glory to God for loving us, leading us, lavishing His blessings upon us, and watching over our journey through life to this point.

Paul said that the Christian has received all spiritual blessings in and through Christ in the heavenly places (Ephesians 1:3). His words are "has blessed," not "will bless." It follows, then, that we should not be asking for more blessings, but for the wisdom to use properly the blessings that we have already been given.

One lady went into a renowned art gallery to view the masterpieces that were hanging there. After looking at one of the famous paintings, she just blurted out without thinking, "I don't see anything to that!" The janitor was nearby and overheard her remark. He retorted, "Don't you wish you could?" It would be a tragedy indeed if we looked back over the way we have come and did not see the Lord's gracious hand upon our lives.

The sad story of the Old Testament is that Israel was blessed of God but she did not acknowledge it; the colossal failure seen in the New Testament is that the Messiah came into the world but His own people did not recognize Him. Let us open our eyes to who Jesus is and what He has done for us. Let us freely acknowledge God's manifold blessings upon our pilgrimage through this world.

Because of His grace, I have been a slave riding on a king's horse at the head of the parade of life. How humbled and grateful I ought to be!

Had it not been for the Lord's lovingkindness and guidance, I shudder to think of where I might be right now. Join with me in praising Him for the wonderful bounties that He has poured out upon us and upon those around us.

Eddie Cloer

"To God and our Savior Jesus Christ be the glory."

*"I am not a citizen of this world trying
to get to heaven; I am a citizen of heaven trying
to get through this world."*

ACKNOWLEDGMENTS

I would like to express my gratitude for those who provided valuable assistance in one way or another with the completion of this book:

To Susan Cloer, my wife, for her invaluable proofing and advice.

To Cheryl Schramm, for her professional proofing, layout, and design.

To Tonda Spiker, for arranging the cover design and other technical matters.

To Wendy Wrigley, for reading the text and making suggestions.

To Gene Cloer, for helping to make sure the dates and facts about the family are correct.

1

HELP FROM GOD'S HAND

*"Have I not commanded you? Be strong and
courageous! Do not tremble or be dismayed, for
the Lord your God is with you wherever you go"
(Joshua 1:9).*

*. . . [F]or He Himself has said, "I will never
desert you, nor will I ever forsake you," so that we
confidently say, "The Lord is my helper, I will not
be afraid, . . ." (Hebrews 13:5, 6).*

Our life stories began with God, and they will end
with God. May we all be wise enough to acknowledge
this reality. God brought us into this world, and He will
be in charge of our exit from it. In addition, He watches
over our journey between birth and death, over the span
of time represented by the two dates that will appear on
our grave markers. He does not put us in this world and
leave us to fend for ourselves. He constantly works to

guide us in the paths of righteousness and to energize us to do His will and His work.

It is a good thing, therefore, to look back and to observe how His hand has led us. Nothing ever just happens in this world: Either God permits it to happen, or He makes it happen. James said that "every good thing given and every perfect gift is from above" (James 1:17). All good things come from God, and, as is stated in James 1:13, all the evil comes from the devil.

It is easier to see the providence of God by looking back over the way we have come than by trying to see it in the present. We know His hand is upon us today, but it is hard to identify what His hand is doing. I hesitate to say that God is doing this or that in my life today, because I am afraid that I will attribute to God something that the devil is doing or that I may attribute to the devil something that God is doing. However, when we review certain events, circumstances, or conversations that led us into the truth and into doing what is right, we can be confident that God was in our midst blessing us.

Looking back over the years of our living brings gratitude and joy, because everywhere we look we see the kindness of God. Standing out clearly from such a panoramic view is the fact that the tender hand of God has been upon us.

We cheerfully acknowledge that the hand that has led us has been a powerful hand. No, we did not see any miracles, miraculous crossings of the Jordan, ax heads floating on water, or healings of the blind or lame; but we did see His providential workings in our behalf. We have no doubt that He has led us.

God worked mighty miracles for all to see at certain times in the Old Testament, and He did so in the New Testament days of our Lord's earthly life and the beginning of the church. We need the records of those miracles, so God gave them to us in the Scriptures. However, now that we have the sacred Scriptures in their completeness, the need for miracles to confirm the gospel no longer exists. God is the same powerful God that He has always been, He just uses His power in a different way. Paul said that He works in us through the same power that He used to raise Jesus from the dead (Ephesians 1:19, 20). The difference is that He works in us providentially, not miraculously.

As we look back, we see His mighty power at work when Daddy survived tuberculosis and my mother kept the family going. We can sing with Hannah:

> "The Lord kills and makes alive;
> He brings down to Sheol and raises up.
> The Lord makes poor and rich;
> He brings low, He also exalts"
>   (1 Samuel 2:6, 7).

We see His power when we observe how we managed to live a good life with almost no income. Somehow we paid all our bills, took care of the necessities of life, and extended a little help to the poor. Once again, the song of Hannah is apropos:

> "Those who were full hire themselves
>   out for bread,
> But those who were hungry cease
>   to hunger.
> Even the barren gives birth to seven,
> But she who has many children languishes"
>   (1 Samuel 2:5).

Although the tuition when I went to Harding was cheaper and the living expenses much less than today, how I got through Harding College is still hard to figure out. One thing I know is that God provided. As a young, seventeen-year-old preacher, I filled in for two weeks for the speaker at the Bentonville, Arkansas, church in the summer of 1962. Someone in that assembly heard those four sermons and decided to send a contribution to me. The donor did not put a return address on the envelope; consequently, I never knew for sure who did it, but what a help that contribution was! It made the difference for my first year at Harding.

These wonders have to be attributed to the power of God. These precious gifts convince us that we will always have enough to do what God wants us to do as long as He wants us to do it.

> "He raises the poor from the dust,
> He lifts the needy from the ash heap
> To make them sit with nobles,
> And inherit a seat of honor;
> For the pillars of the earth are the Lord's,
> And He set the world on them"
>   (1 Samuel 2:8).

Further, we recognize His hand as being a faithful hand. We have found Him to be true to His Word. He has not always answered our prayers the way that we thought He would. In fact, sometimes we were not able to tell how He answered our prayers; but we knew He did, for we walked by faith, and not by sight (2 Corinthians 5:7).

> "There is no one holy like the Lord,
> Indeed, there is no one besides You,
> Nor is there any rock like our God"
>   (1 Samuel 2:2).

The beauty of walking with God is the realization that you are walking with Someone who will never lie to you and who will keep every promise He has made to you. We have not always been able to trace His hand, but we have always been able to trust His heart.

> The hand with which He works never fails,
> The pen with which He writes never blots,
> And the tongue with which He speaks
>   never slips.

In an uncertain world, how wonderful it is to rest your case upon the unerring faithfulness of God!

We certainly know that His hand has been a gracious hand. He rescued us from sin and set our feet on the old "S & N"—the strait and narrow road that leads to eternal glory—and we have been walking that road ever since (Matthew 7:14; Luke 13:24; KJV). Several have walked that road on into glory, but several of us are still walking it, trudging along, seeing by the eye of faith in the distance a city whose builder and maker is God.

Our journey has not been in a straight line, for it has zigged and zagged, with a mistake and a correction, with more mistakes and more corrections. Our Christian lives are a living testimony to the amazing grace of God. How thankful we are that God has answered us according to His lovingkindness and not according to our sins! He has been patient with us, giving us time to catch on, time to understand, and opportunities to correct our foolish ways. I can thankfully say that some growth in the Christian virtues has taken place. We are not what we were, and we believe that we will not be tomorrow what we are today.

> "He keeps the feet of His godly ones,
> But the wicked ones are silenced
>   in darkness;
> For not by might shall a man prevail"
>   (1 Samuel 2:9).

The gospel came at first to our house when Dad and Mother started attending worship services at the Sonora schoolhouse in 1936. A wonderful Christian man, James L. Neal, a rural mail carrier and a personal evangelist par excellence, noticed that Dad and Mother might be good prospects for gospel teaching. He asked a young preacher by the name of Joe Spaulding to visit with them and urge them to come to the Sunday afternoon services at the wood-framed schoolhouse. On a Sunday afternoon in September 1936, after a meal in our home, Joe asked them to become Christians. They made the decision to begin their Christian life, and Joe, at that time a nineteen-year-old preacher, took them to Flanigan's Lake nearby and baptized them. From that event, the gospel has gradually moved to the rest of us.

> "My heart exults in the Lord; . . .
> . . . Because I rejoice in Your salvation"
>   (1 Samuel 2:1).

No one of us would claim to know all of the marvelous ways that God works in the lives of people. However, we can be sure that behind the curtain of what we can see, behind the veil of the physical eyesight, God wondrously and providentially has guided us into His way and truth.

Faith is not a special, sentimental feeling about God that sweeps over us every once in a while; it is not a tearful appreciation of God that overwhelms us on rare occasions. Faith is the most matter-of-fact, down-to-earth attitude that one can contemplate. It rests squarely upon what God has said (Romans 10:17). It is not just mulling over and thinking about what God has stated; it accepts His Word and acts upon it in trust and love. Having seen and heard what God has said in the Scriptures, faith takes a stand on what God has revealed through an act of will, choosing to walk as He has commanded us to walk. The subject of faith can be boiled down to a way of life for a person who, by his intellect and emotions, has chosen to put the weight of his or her life and eternity upon what God has said. Such a person lives by God's precepts and trusts in the promises that He has clearly made known to us in the Scriptures.

Dad and Mother chose to accept the testimony of God's Word and set out to be what it prescribes for one to be. As we saw them making the path of faith the pattern of their lives, we were inspired to choose the same path.

God has kept His promises to us. He has loved us, led us, and lavished His blessings upon us. Day by day we have received help from His hand. We can assuredly say with Samuel of old, "Thus far the Lord has helped us."

"We cannot always trace God's hand,
but we can always trust His heart."

2

MY EARLIEST MEMORIES

Then Samuel took a stone and set it between
Mizpah and Shen, and named it Ebenezer, saying,
"Thus far the Lord has helped us" (1 Samuel 7:12).

My mother was thirty-nine when I was born. My parents could well have named me "No-more," for I was the last of five children with whom God blessed them. At least, they regarded us as blessings, even though many times, I fear, we were burdens and blisters to them.

How Dad and Mother managed to rear us is still a great mystery to all of us. While in his late twenties, my father came down with tuberculosis, a terrible disease that had already taken the lives of his father and one of his sisters. Treatment for TB was in its infancy in those days, and the only hope for Daddy's survival while in his thirties was for him to be confined to a bed for two years in a sanatorium at Booneville, Arkansas. Mother was left alone to look after three young boys who were 5, 10, and 12. My sister and I had not come along as yet.

No one really knows how she handled everything. I heard her discuss those years, but I do not remember ever hearing her complain about them. If, at the Judgment, God hands out "medals for mothers," I am sure she will get one. With little education, she had to use her head and reach deep within for the rugged determination that was required. Sacrificing herself for her children had to be the order of the day. Our relatives could provide little help for this wife and mother in distress; but with the assistance and encouragement of friends—and especially by God's grace and providence—she eked out a living, providing at least shelter, the basic needs, and love. I am sure those years that Dad was confined to bed either at home or at Booneville dragged on as if the years were going to be a never-ending saga of sickness. Surely, this time must have been one of the darkest times of her life. Many families lived amid hard and harsh times in those years, but it seems that Dad and Mother faced far more than their share of trials.

At my birth, unknown to me, the songs of patriotism were in the air. World War II was being fought in Germany, France, and Japan, in answer to what Hitler, the mad man, wanted to do to the world. The youths of the land were being drafted for military duty, and some young men from our community were sacrificed on the "altar of freedom." The precious things of life always come at a dear price.

I have few memories from the early years of my life, as is the case with most people; but some have weathered the years. Those memories that remain still sparkle like diamonds in my heart.

There is the memory of worship. Although we lived six and a half miles from Springdale, Arkansas, where our membership was with the South Thompson Street church of Christ, we drove to almost every worship service in our old, beat-up pickup truck.

It is said that one can trace the journeys of Abraham by following the smoke of the altars that he had built. Everywhere he went, he would first of all build an altar and worship. I cannot remember a time when we did not go to worship. Pity the children who must grow up without the blessed memory of going to worship regularly, as a family. Those trips to be a part of the worship of the church put something into my childish mind— notably, that worship is important. Those experiences taught me the great scriptural truth that worship is to be put at the head of the list of the things we *must* do, regardless of our circumstances.

There is the memory of sympathy for bumps, bruises, and a broken heart. One could not grow up in Northwest Arkansas and not develop early a love for horses. They were used for plowing, riding, and a host of other things. Tractors were beginning to show up here and there, but most of the plowing by the small farmers was being done with horses or mules. We had two horses—a gentle, lovable one and a self-willed, unfriendly one. It didn't take me long to become fast friends with the gentle one. We called him Rex. He was more than a horse to me; he was a big, dear, lovable friend, maybe like a teddy bear to some children.

When the workday was over, the horses were unhitched from the double shovel and turned toward the barn. Occasionally, Dad would hoist me up and allow me to ride Rex to the barn. I was like a flea on an elephant's ear. That horse took a little boy and made him a king for a few moments. Because of the gentle spirit Rex had, it was safe for me to ride him. That ride was always the delight of my day.

One day weary Rex forgot about having me aboard, and he stopped at the ford for a drink of water before Daddy could warn me. I went over his head into the mud and rocks, and I still carry a faint scar on my eyebrow from that fall. Did that tragedy cause me to hate Rex? No way. "He didn't mean it. He was just tired and forgot. After all, a friend won't betray a friend," I thought.

One memory of Rex remains vividly planted in my mind: It was Rex's departure. The veterinarian said that his days were numbered, and Daddy had to send him away. I remember pressing my nose to one of the windows in the front of our house and watching in tears as they took Rex in the back of a big truck up the hill and off to become glue, as I later found out. My mother tried to console me with the tender words "God is going to give us something better." My childish mind had no theology in it; I had only emptiness in my boyish heart for my dear friend, Rex. Her words have stayed with me, however. Later in life, I would learn the meaning of Romans 8:28 and would understand more about how God often turns a tragedy into a triumph. As I look back, I realize that God replaced Rex with a tractor, something badly needed by Daddy and something absolutely necessary if he planned to continue to farm for a living.

There is the memory of a two-room schoolhouse. Education in those days came through little schoolhouses scattered throughout the communities. They were close to people's homes, small in size, and served as sort of a focal point of each community. These schools might have two teachers, but some of them had only one. The teachers taught everything—spelling, English, math, science, history, etc. Dad usually took us to school in the morning, but we walked home in the evening. Around 3:30 in the afternoon, the roads were dotted with children, sometimes running and sometimes walking as they made their way home. Sometimes we got into trouble, but most of the time it was just happy, memorable fellowship.

Then, there is the memory of unconditional love. We did not have a lot in the way of earthly goods. We always looked forward to getting a new pair of shoes—one pair that was supposed to last us all year. If the sole came loose before the year was out, we could always wire it together and get a little more wear out of it. Clothes were few, but we used well what we had. We wore them until they just could not be worn anymore. Most people in our community had more possessions and luxuries than we had, but no one outdistanced us in love. There was always a lavish helping to go around. No child was elevated above the others, and no child was accidentally left behind.

One man said to a father of an incorrigible son: "If he were my son, I'd disinherit him." "So would I," answered the old father, "if he were *your* son—but he's my son, you see!" When we made mistakes, Dad and Mother believed in applying the board of education to the seat of learning; but there was never a question about their love for us, regardless of what we did.

Think about these early memories of mine. What should parents provide for their children? What would be the bottom line, the essentials? In this age of materialism and affluence, most believe that parents must provide the finest in things for their children—that is, possessions, conveniences, and the like—but is this really true? Look at these memories: Are they not the essentials for children in any home—worship, sympathy, an education, and unconditional love? Did I really miss out on anything? It seems to me that the neglected child is the one who does not have these essentials, regardless of whatever else he or she may have.

Dare I not see the hand of God in all of this? He provided what I needed when I needed it. Remember, God will meet *our need*, but He does not set out to satisfy *our greed*.

Maybe you should pause and thank God for giving you the essentials by giving you parents who saw through the nonessentials and, during tough times or good times, saw to it that you always had the necessities of life.

The Lord has led us and has brought us to this juncture in our journey. With confident faith, we look to the "God of the hitherto" to be the "God of the henceforth." As He graciously led us through yesterday, He will go before us and lovingly guide us and give us what we need through all the tomorrows that may come.

∾

"There are some things from our past that we should trash, and there are some things that we should treasure."

"God will meet our need, but He does not promise to satisfy our greed."

3

THE GIFTS MY PARENTS GAVE ME

But if anyone does not provide for his own, and especially for those of his household, he has denied the faith and is worse than an unbeliever (1 Timothy 5:8).

My Dad had the benefit of only a ninth-grade, public education; my mother was able to go through high school and a business college. However, each of them acquired a PhD degree from the University of Practical Experience, graduating from it with honors in their mid-fifties. They wrote their dissertations day by day on the pages of our hearts and theirs, and their work was reviewed continually by the professional committee of the harsh realities of life, with the head of their committee being Dr. Wisdom. Dad specialized in grit, discipline, and willpower. Mother focused on love, compassion, and the ability "to be there" for anyone in her family who needed her. They graduated from the university quietly, without any celebration or fanfare. I was not even aware that they possessed PhD's until I had left home in the 1960s and reflected on how I had been influenced by them.

One thing that convinced me of the depth of their understanding of life was when I took notice of what they had given me. It requires a lot of wisdom and good, sanctified judgment to give our children what they need instead of what they want. Dad and Mother had what it takes, and they gave us the important values that the world most often overlooks. They did not give us much in the way of material goods and special favors, but what they did give us far outweighed the gifts of dollars, trinkets, land, and houses.

What did they give us?

They gave us roots. Of course, they gave us a sense of belonging in the Cloer family. We knew who we were, and we were happy about it. They did not foster vain arrogance or sensual pride in us, but they did cultivate in us a wholesome identity.

I saw Dad make sacrifices just for the preservation of our name. If someone understood that he had made a promise, he went ahead and kept that promise—even if they had completely misunderstood him—so that he would not be perceived as being dishonest. To him, being honest was absolutely essential. He did not see honesty as the best policy; he saw honesty as a necessary part of Christian living. It was not optional; it was obligatory.

Further, our parents introduced us to the Lord's church, the highest and greatest extended family there is. This introduction gave us an even greater feeling of belonging. They loved the church and sought to be nothing more and nothing less than the church that Jesus built on the Day of Pentecost after His resurrection.

One of the delights of Dad's life was assisting Harbert W. Hooker with his tent meetings in Northwest Arkansas. Daddy often said that, for teaching a small audience, brother Hooker was one of the finest preachers he had ever heard. With a detailed chart before the assembly, a rapid-fire delivery, and a keen intellect, brother Hooker could preach as no one else could. In just a little over a year, ten to fifteen churches were established in Northwest Arkansas through his tent meetings. Those churches remain, for the most part, until today. Dad witnessed close up as the gospel was preached by this great preacher, and he beheld churches emerging into existence as a result of that preaching. That experience did something for Daddy. It put in him a belief in the power of the gospel to make Christians and to make churches of Christ, and he passed that important belief on to the rest of us.

Thus we learned early in our home that the only way to be a true New Testament Christian is by carefully following the gospel of the New Testament. The only creed that a Christian has is his New Testament.

Through the fellowship of the church family, we were privileged to know great men and women of God and tremendous preachers. That was a blessed experience that we will treasure for the duration of our lives.

The Jews in the Old Testament regarded all the children, regardless of the family from which they came, as being the children of the religious community. They belonged to the community of believers, and every older one in that community had a responsibility toward all the children as if they were his own physical children. That was the type of belonging I felt as I grew up. I belonged not only to my physical family, but also to a wonderful spiritual family. Both families claimed me, and both families looked after me. Their care and concern for me gave me a deep sense of roots.

They gave us wings. At the appropriate time, and at a time we thought best, our parents were willing to let go of us and let us pursue our own lives. They kept us in their hearts, but they opened the nest and let us fly away.

I remember the day that I left home for the last time. I was moving to Clarksville, Arkansas, to be the local preacher. I was twenty-two, single, and eager to move into my own work for the Lord. Mother did not say anything, but I noticed out of the corner of my eye that when my back was turned she was wiping away the tears. I was the last child to leave, and she knew that her home would be different from then on.

As the freshman students at Harding University get ready to return home for the Thanksgiving holidays, I try to tell them that they cannot "go home again." They look at me with an empty stare, and some of them get misty-eyed, but they know that I am right. I am trying to brace them for the new relationship they will enter with their parents. When they return home, they will see a different home. It is more than the fact that younger brothers or sisters have already moved into their rooms. They will see something far more important occurring—they will observe that their parents have given them freedom to begin sprouting wings.

Pity the young person who is kept penned up by the home from which he came and is never allowed to fly. I remember having a young lady in my Bible class whom I had known through the years. She confided in me one day that her dad called every other night. I asked her, "What does he say?" She said, "He wants me to come home." Can you imagine a young lady trying to over-come homesickness when her dad is calling every other night pleading for her to come home? I felt sorry for this freshman, because I could see that her dad was refusing to give her the freedom she needed to become an adult. He had probably given her roots, but he could not give her wings. She lasted only one semester, and then she went home to stay.

Life says, "Blessed are the parents who give their children wings, for they shall be blessed with the knowledge that they have allowed their children to grow up."

They gave us a map. They put in our hands the Word of God, the sacred Scriptures, and taught us that the Bible is the truth of heaven and should be faithfully followed. They believed that the Bible was the only map that can guide us safely through the wilderness of this world.

Daddy freely admitted to me that there were many questions about spiritual matters that he could not answer. He read the Bible often, but he did not consider himself a Bible scholar. He enjoyed listening to great preaching, and he enjoyed a well-taught Bible class; but he knew that he had not arrived in his understanding of the Scriptures.

However, certain truths always came through loud and clear in our conversations—the Scriptures are inspired of God, they are true and accurate, and they are the only safe guide in life. I do not remember ever hearing him say anything or even imply anything that would be derogatory to the integrity of the Scriptures.

When I started preaching, Dad would often tell me about a theme that he wished I would prepare a sermon on, and then he would say, "People need to hear what the Bible says about that." He wanted me to preach the Bible and only the Bible, and he wanted people to understand what the Bible taught.

I remember the last time that I saw Dad when he was conscious. He had leukemia. Over the painful months, it had finally brought him down to death's door, and he knew it. I had agreed to hold a gospel meeting in Bentonville, Arkansas, just so that I could be near him during his final days. I went by on Wednesday evening before the last service to see him. He was in pain, discouraged, and thinking about the life beyond. I asked him how he was doing, and he pointed upward and said, "I'm ready to pass over there." He said, "Would you read to me the passage where Paul spoke of departing to be with Christ?" I knew the passage that he meant, for we had talked about it before. I could not read it because of my tears, so I wound up just quoting it:

> But if I am to live on in the flesh, this will mean fruitful labor for me; and I do not know which to choose. But I am hard-pressed from both directions, having the desire to depart and be with Christ, for that is very much better; yet to remain on in the flesh is more necessary for your sake (Philippians 1:22–24).

I visited with him a little more after sharing the passage, but I could tell that he was tired and weary. We prayed together, and I went on to the meeting. I went back by the hospital after the service, but he was sleeping and I did not wake him. I returned to Scarcy to teach my Bible classes, hoping that I could see him again on the weekend. He went into unconsciousness before I could go back to be with him; consequently, we will not talk again until we meet on the other side of death. The last memory

I have of Dad is that of a man who was relying upon the Scriptures to tell him what to expect in the future.

Both Dad and Mom knew that there was only one book, the book we call the Bible, that could see us to our eternal home. They put it into our hands as a map for life.

I know that much responsibility rests upon me, for I must decide what I will do with the roots, the wings, and the map. However, if my life is a failure, it will not be one because my parents did not provide for me what every set of parents ought to give their children—a sense of belonging, freedom to live our own lives, and the light of the Scriptures for our paths.

"One can be educated beyond his intelligence; and one can have little education yet possess the wisdom of a PhD."

4

REMEMBERING MY MOTHER

Charm is deceitful and beauty is vain,
But a woman who fears the Lord,
She shall be praised (Proverbs 31:30).

My mother feared the Lord. With respect for God and all mothers, I would like to tell of her excellent qualities.

The easiest task in the world for anyone to do is to give thanks to God for his or her mother. This prayer of gratitude is a delightful duty for two reasons. For one thing, our mothers shouldered the brunt of getting us started in life. They carried us approximately nine months before our births, and then they walked through the house of pain and touched lightly the door of death to bring us into the world. Furthermore, after our entrance into the world, they took us wherever they went for two or three years, and probably physically carried us most of the time! We could truthfully write above the first years of our lives the telling caption "When I Was Carried by My Mother." Our fathers helped with the beginning of our days, but we all know that our mothers tended to the bigger part of that beginning.

The most helpless living creature on earth is a newborn baby. An infant calf can stand, walk, and seek sustenance the first day of his life. A colt wobbles, walks, and runs his first day on earth; but a human infant just wiggles, stares, cries, and depends totally on his or her kindhearted mother to manage his or her life. For days and months after our births, our mothers fed us, bathed us, burped us, and put us to bed. Actually, there is a sense in which it can be said that all of us are "our mother's children."

In addition, after we were on our own for a while, we came back to our mothers for the encouragement, warmth, and confidence that only a mother can give. Even grown men have to admit that they depend on their mothers. There is something that they give us that no one else can. All of us would agree with Franklin Camp, who wrote shortly after the death of his mother, "The world is a strange and different place after one's mother dies." We have a continuing relationship with our mothers that we have with no other person; when they leave us, the world looks much different to us. They bring to this place called Earth—which, at times, is an unfriendly, rugged, dismal place—an assurance for our hearts, a laughter over our mistakes, plus a happiness and a peace for our souls.

Although, in the main, all mothers have these same adorable traits, every mother possesses a remarkable uniqueness about her that springs up from her personality, abilities, education, and background. For example, in Jochebed, Moses' mother (Exodus 2:2–5; Hebrews 11:23), we see an enduring faith; in Ruth, Obed's mother (Ruth 1:16, 17), we see the beauty of loyalty; from Mary (Luke 1:38), the earthly mother of Jesus, comes a picture of submission to God; from Lois (2 Timothy 1:5), the mother of Timothy, comes the stern charge to teach our children God's Word.

Every mother has her own strengths and weaknesses, but because of the close relationship that we have sustained with our mothers, we tend to remember only their admirable qualities and nothing of their failures. At least, I have a blind spot regarding my mother's weaknesses. I do not remember any foibles that my mother had. I know that she was not perfect, but her memory is just a beautiful, dear memory of what she did for me.

When I think of my mother, I think of a quiet, faithful Christian woman. She became a Christian alongside Dad when she was thirty-one. So far as I know, she never taught a Bible class, but she loved the Lord and His church and was involved in the work of the church in numerous ways. Her expertise was visiting the sick and watching over them until they were well.

When I think of my mother, I think of a hard-working person with gentle hands and a tender heart. Mother was a rather quiet person who was ceaselessly working. She illustrated this old adage:

> Man works from sun to sun,
> But a woman's work is never done.

The dairy farm on which we lived was not big enough to sustain us, and mother had to take a job at a canning factory in Springdale. Canning factories did not need people with an education; they just needed someone who could help peel tomatoes or snap beans, and my mother could. I never went inside the factory where she worked, but I was told that it was an assembly line, a monotonous arrangement. Workers were paid by the hour, plus a little above the hourly wage if the quota was exceeded. Like the worthy woman of Proverbs 31, my mother was a busy woman:

> She stretches out her hands to the distaff,
> And her hands grasp the spindle (Proverbs 31:19).

By working at the canning factory, Mother demonstrated the kind of woman she was. If extra money was needed for our family, she would do the work to get it, regardless of the kind of work it was.

When I think of my mother, I think of good food and meaningful fellowship. Mother loved to cook, and she especially loved to cook for her family. I believe it was her way of giving a beautiful blessing to us. Even when the men and the boys of the household arose at some unearthly hour to go fishing, go deer hunting, or leave on a necessary trip, she would awaken before they did and would have breakfast cooked and ready to serve when they woke up. The aroma of freshly baked biscuits and frying bacon magnetically drew us into the kitchen.

The wonderful woman of Proverbs 31 is acclaimed because she arose before daylight and prepared breakfast for her family.

> She rises also while it is still night,
> And gives food to her household, . . .
>   (Proverbs 31:15).

Some of our happiest times were spent as a family around the kitchen table, enjoying a good meal and entering into the fellowship that would always accompany it. Sometimes our discussions were light and frivolous, sometimes they were more on the thought-provoking side, sometimes they were about the events of the day, and sometimes they were just about what was going on with us. They were always the centerpiece of wonderful family comradeship.

When anyone came for a visit, we treated the guests as royally as we could. Mother provided the best meal within her power, and Dad carried on interesting conversation with them. It just fell the lot of my mother to prepare the meals, and she always gladly did it. When company came, we were like Abraham when the three special visitors came to see him: We ran to my mother and asked her to put some food on the table.

> So Abraham hurried into the tent to Sarah, and said,
> "Quickly, prepare three measures of fine flour, knead
> it, and make bread cakes" (Genesis 18:6).

My mother never complained about preparing the meals. I believe she saw a meal as a lovely gift that she could give her family.

When I think of my mother, I think of daily kindnesses that made life cleaner and easier. Mother wanted me to be clean and well-groomed, and she wanted me wearing freshly washed clothes. Those are good rules to go by, I would say. Making sure that our clothes were washed and ready for wearing was just something that she quietly did. The virtuous woman of Proverbs 31 gave special attention to the clothes her family wore:

> She is not afraid of the snow for her household,
> For all her household are clothed with scarlet
>   (Proverbs 31:21).

The woman of whom this writer spoke clothed her family in the finest clothes. My mother could not put us in the most expensive clothes, but she kept us in clean clothes. I think she believed that clean clothes would help us to have confidence in ourselves in public; and she just believed that a decent, God-fearing person should be clean and neat.

Think about the continual kindnesses expressed to us by our mothers and wives. These mementos of love are evident to us every day, if we will only take the time to notice them. Each morning we see that a diligent hand has done a helpful deed for us. Every time we open a drawer, every time we go to the closet, we see the result of the work that someone did to make our lives a little easier and nicer.

When I think of my mother, I think of forgiveness and acceptance. I knew that regardless of the mistakes I had made, I would continue to be loved by my mother. God made mothers with a tremendous capacity to love even an unlovable child. Rudyard Kipling captured this thought in his poem "Mother O' Mine":

> If I were hanged on the highest hill,
> Mother o' mine, O mother o' mine!
> I know whose love would follow me still,
> Mother o' mine, O mother o' mine!
>
> If I were drowned in the deepest sea,
> Mother o' mine, O mother o' mine!

I know whose tears would come down to me,
Mother o' mine, O mother o' mine!

If I were damned of body and soul,
I know whose prayers would make me whole,
Mother o' mine, O mother o' mine!

Later, when I began preaching and my mother was in the assembly, I could rest assured that regardless of how poorly I preached the precious gospel, I would have one person in the congregation who would appreciate my efforts. She always listened attentively, and she always sought to encourage me.

Someone has said that every preacher will have a Corinth, a congregation riddled with problems that demands much from him; so, every preacher needs a Philippi, a sweetheart type of congregation that continually supports him and holds him up before God in prayer. God knew that we would have our "Corinth" days—days that drain us, days when problem after problem comes down on us. That is why He gave us a "Philippi" person, a mother, who sees us for what we can be, who just loves us with no hidden agendas.

To me, my mother was a rare and beautiful woman. Her hands were rough because of a skin condition, and her physical frame was bent because of years of work, but to me she was lovely. She was at the center of many a happy meal that was surrounded by sweet, memorable fellowship. She expressed to us daily kindnesses with her continual care for our personal needs. She showered us with an accepting love. She wanted us to do better and sought to improve us, but she always took us as we were and where we were and just loved us, leaving the work of transforming us to God and His Word.

One of the pioneer preachers said that on one occasion he was somewhat ashamed of his mother. She had come into a crowd of his friends, and he was sort of forced to introduce her to them. He said that she was not educated and had worked as a day-laborer for many years. Her hands had grown rough, and her skin was leathery and weather-worn because of her being out in the fields so much. After her death, he said he was haunted by that moment when he was embarrassed to make her known to some of his friends. As he thought about what she had done for him and how she had done so much with what she had, he was smitten with godly repentance over his terrible mistreatment of her. He said, "When I get to heaven, I will walk up before the angels and all the redeemed, the greatest audience on earth or in heaven, put my arm around her, and announce for all to hear, 'This is my mother!'"

I loved my mother while she was here. I was never ashamed of her, and my heart wells up with gratitude for all that she did for me. She bore the strains and stresses, the defeats and the victories of life so well. I am deeply sorry that I could not do more for her. I, too, would relish the opportunity to walk before the heavenly hosts, hug her, and say to God's court, "This woman is my mother!"

"A home that has two heads but no heart is a monstrosity."

5

DADDY'S SERMON

Fathers, do not provoke your children to anger, but bring them up in the discipline and instruction of the Lord (Ephesians 6:4).

Hear, O sons, the instruction of a father, And give attention that you may gain understanding (Proverbs 4:1).

My dad was a farmer. He made his living by working with the earth, and that kind of life gave him a fascination and love for the outdoors. If he had to take a trip across the country, he always wanted to drive instead of fly; he wanted to see the countryside, the houses, and the cities from the highways and not from the air. Much of his life was lived in the sunshine, out in the fields and on the hills. He loved to be near water, and he wanted to be surrounded by cattle, fish, deer, and all the animals and birds of the woods and meadows. He saw the world of nature up close. This "down to earth" lifestyle affected his attitude and thinking toward people and things. It showed in his face, in his callused hands, and in his appreciation for the country. The farm was his life, his livelihood, and his love.

He and Mother acquired the forty-acre farm where I grew up for the back taxes owed on it in 1940. The farm was composed of a "bunch of hills" and two bottoms near the creek, which we called the big and little bottoms. These bottoms were the little flat lands where we grew corn, hay, beans, wheat, and grain sorghum for silage. When I was young, I told Daddy that I needed a field of concentration for growth and learning, and he agreed: He gave me each summer these two bottoms to weed with a hoe and my hands. It did not take me long to decide that farming would not be my occupation in life, if I had anything to say about it!

In the 1950s Dad turned the farm into a dairy farm. His herd grew until he was milking around thirty mixed cows—Jerseys, Guernseys, Holsteins, and Brown Swiss. The life of a dairy farmer was arduous and confining. Every morning and evening the cows were brought in, milked, and fed. Those chores had to be done regardless of rain, snow, sunshine, sickness, or health. If we did not go to get the cows, they came to get us. There were no vacations or days off. The work was persistent, perpetual, and demanding.

Since Daddy did most of the work on the farm himself, eventually dairy farming became too much for his health, and he turned the farm into a small beef ranch. Shortly before he died, I asked him if he would pursue the same route he had taken with the farm if he had his life to live over again. He answer quickly, "No, I believe that I would have gone the beef cattle route sooner and would have gotten a job of some kind in town. With that arrangement we could have made out better financially and it would not have been such a strain on me."

The farm did not support Dad and Mother well, so there were always decisions to make about what we could buy and what we would have to skip until the next year. However, they managed to live a good life with what they had. They were generous and big-hearted even though they did not have much to live on.

When Daddy became a Christian, he wanted to be just a member of the church that Jesus had built and nothing more. Denominationalism had no attraction for him at all. He despised insincerity. He did not have much patience with someone who wanted to be religious but not righteous, someone who was sentimental but not saintly, or someone who claimed to have faith in God but would ignore what God had said in His Word.

Daddy had no experience in preaching. When I began preaching, he could not really tell me much about preaching other than what he had observed, read, and heard. However, the advice he gave me was always sound, wise, and worth considering by anyone who is trying to preach God's message publicly. I took to heart whatever he said.

I know that, during the latter part of his life, Daddy made some short talks on Wednesday nights; but I was never privileged to hear any of them. I was out of the home by then, and he never gave one of them when I was home visiting. In rummaging through the effects that he left behind, I found notes of his that were obviously used for those talks. Even though he was not a preacher per se, apparently he could make effective little presentations on God's Word when the need arose or when he was asked to make one.

However, in another sense Daddy was a preacher, a good preacher. He was a preacher in the sense of his daily living, the sense in which all of us are preachers. Daddy preached with his actions, his attitudes, and the direction that he decided to go with his life. The sermon he preached through the way he lived, I believe, was a strong sermon in several ways. It was a proclamation of truth to all of us that will stay with us until our lives end on this earth or until the Lord comes.

In that sermon, he said that life does not mean much unless one is a Christian. We had happy times as a family, to be sure, but if you were to remove Christ and His church from those days when we were growing up, there would be a huge hole of emptiness and despair. A family without Christ is not much of a family. If you take God out of the word "good," you have only an "o" left, and that is about the way it is when it comes to life without God; it is a zero, a doughnut.

Daddy insisted on our going to Bible class and worship regularly. Making those trips to Springdale were hard for him because of the demands the farm made on him, but he always took us without any reservation. He saw the need for it, and going to Bible study and worship became a part of his life and ours.

Paul said, "For to me, to live is Christ and to die is gain" (Philippians 1:21). If you removed Christ from Paul's statement, you would not have much left. You would certainly have to leave out "gain," and then you just have "For me to live is to die." What a gloomy picture of life that is! Daddy saw much more to life than just "buying time" or "treading water" until it was time to die!

In the sermon that Daddy lived, he said that sometimes life requires grit, fortitude, and gumption. We really wondered how Daddy overcame some of the difficulties he faced. While battling TB, he underwent an operation on his lung without his being put to sleep. He told me that the morning before that operation was the longest morning he had ever lived. He came out of his battle with TB with a damaged lung that would not function much at all, yet he could out-work and out-walk almost any man.

What do you do when life is really tough? How do you handle a blizzard of hardships, a storm of adversity? Daddy would say that you turn your face to it, reach down inside your soul, bring up the strength that you never knew you had, and ask God to stand beside you. Then, you tell the blizzard, "Come on, but make sure you are armed and ready for a fight, because I am going to give you one!" Daddy did not know how to say, "I quit!" He was like the little crawfish that had gotten out of the water and had crawled onto a railroad track. As the big locomotive came speeding down the track, the little crawfish was last seen trying to reach up and pinch the bumper guard of the engine. He went out with vision and ambition. He died challenging a locomotive to a duel!

The Christian's plea is never impotence. He does not say regarding any holy enterprise, "I can't do that!" His plea is always omnipotence. With confident faith he says, "I can do all things through Christ who will strengthen me." The Christian wins over life with spiritual willpower: He provides the will, and Christ provides the power.

In the sermon that Daddy preached with his life, he said that it is important for one to learn to give. The amount one gives is not what matters most; the supreme thing is learning that part of the Christian's personality is possessing a love that gives. Every Sunday morning, Daddy gave. When special needs arose, Daddy gave. He knew that one can give without loving but one cannot love without giving.

When I attended the graduate school, I chose to support myself for most of my schooling. I did not ask for a scholarship from the school until the last year I was there. I knew if I was granted a scholarship, someone else would have to pay for it, so I decided to try to provide for my own graduate education in the Scriptures.

I was preaching for a small congregation, and the support that they gave me was limited. My wife, Susan, and I had decided that we would live on what I received. She was teaching school, but we were trying to save what she made. With no children at that time, we thought we could handle our living expenses in this way. Above paying my bill at the graduate school, we gave a good contribution each Sunday to the church of which we were a part. One day as I sat in class, I looked at the young man next to me, who was attending the graduate school on total scholarships. I thought, "Someone is helping him go to school so that he can be a better preacher and whoever is supporting him is considering their help as a contribution to the Lord. Why can't I do the same? Why can't I consider my tuition and other expenses for my graduate work a contribution to the Lord and cut back on our contribution to the church?" I made the mistake of mentioning this question to Daddy. Quick as a flash, he said, "You can't give to yourself!"

What he said has stayed with me. At first, his words stung like a bee sting, but then they lingered in my mind and helped straighten out my thinking. His words were a valuable lesson to me on giving to the Lord. His point was that a portion of all we make should be given to the church or to good works that are separate and apart from our personal activities and ambitions. In Daddy's mind, that type of giving was the kind that constituted Christian giving. This view was not only Daddy's doctrine, but it was also his practice.

Daddy's sermon taught us that one needs to be faithful to the end. It was clear to all of us that Daddy would be faithful to Christ to the end of his earthly life. As the end drew near, we were privileged to behold the culmination of a life spent in dedication to spiritual things. He knew that one could be put out on third base, that one could have a shipwreck coming into the dock, that one could have an accident only a mile from home; so he was diligent about his relationship with God in his last days.

One of the last touching memories I have of Dad was the correction of some wrong he had committed. He felt that he had offended a neighbor. I do not know what he had done. I did not ask. He told me that he needed to straighten out something with a neighbor and wondered if I would go to his house and ask him to come by for a few minutes. Daddy was in his last stages with leukemia. I went over to the neighbor's house and asked him to come by. When he arrived, I took him to Daddy's bedroom, closed the door, and left them alone. I am sure that Daddy apologized to him, and they prayed together. Daddy wanted to settle that matter before he died, and I am sure he did. After the visit with his neighbor, he had peace about that mistake he had made. He knew this truth:

> Nothing is ever settled until it is settled right, nothing is ever settled right until it is settled with God, nothing is ever settled with God until it is settled God's way, and nothing is ever settled God's way until it is settled according to the teachings of the New Testament.

Yes, from one viewpoint, Daddy was a preacher. "Be a Christian, live with determination, be generous, be faithful to the end": Those are the particulars that stand out in my mind from his sermon.

I have heard some great sermons during my lifetime, but Daddy's sermon was more effective than most of them for two reasons. First, it was meaningful to us because we *saw* it. It was paraded before us in the middle of the drama of life. We received a close-up, living color, in the flesh, personal viewing of it. Truly, a sermon needs to be heard, but it is especially important for the sermons preached to the family by the parents to be seen. The old line "I'd rather see a sermon than hear one any day" perhaps should be altered for the family so that it reads "Children need to see a sermon from their parents every day, as well as hear one."

Second, Daddy's sermon was a good one because it has had *staying power*. Some sermons are heard and forgotten; but other sermons become a part of you, for they enter your spirit and help to shape your personality and conduct. His sermon placed its imprint upon my soul, and it still makes a daily contribution to what I am.

If you ask me, Daddy's sermon was a powerful spiritual lesson, and any family is blessed indeed to see that kind of sermon in its leader. As I walk by the door of the auditorium of life, I can look back at what I have heard and seen and say to my dad, "That was a good sermon. It will challenge and change me from now on. Thank you for it."

∽∾

"It is a wonderful thing when a boy can see his heavenly Father through his earthly dad."

6

COMING TO CHRIST
IN MY YOUTH

And coming to Him as to a living stone which has been rejected by men, but is choice and precious in the sight of God (1 Peter 2:4).

Fairly early in life, a young man realizes that he must take charge of his life by consciously pointing it to the destination to which it should go. He must make the decision according to his best understanding, and he must make the choice as an individual standing alone before God. He realizes that he can no longer blame or praise others for what he is, since he is becoming solely responsible for what his life is going to be. Friends and loved ones may have assisted him by preparing him for the significant decision he is making, and they may even stand by him with words of encouragement when the decision is made. The crucial part, the actual making of the decision in the sacred palace of the soul, rests upon his shoulders and upon them alone.

On a much higher level, but during a similar time that is fraught with mystery, Jesus—at the age of twelve—said to His mother, "Why did you seek Me? Did you not know that I must be about my Father's business?" (Luke 2:49; NKJV). He had emerged from childhood with a resolute head regarding the road His life would take. After this trip to Jerusalem, He would continue to be subject to His parents; but the direction that His life would go had been clearly marked by this choice that He had made.

I was eleven years of age when I decided to become a Christian. Perhaps no memory from my youthful days is as clearly etched in my mind as this one. I remember what I was thinking at the time of the choice, and I remember in detail the events that surrounded my actual obedience to the gospel. What the preacher said, what others did, and the encouragement of my parents will linger with me as long as I live.

A family can do just so much to help a young man take this important step, inasmuch as it must be fully and finally his decision. My family and friends gave me what they could, and I made the decision in July 1955 during a gospel meeting in Springdale, Arkansas. Of course, I am glad I made the decision. Who would not be? I have never heard of anyone who sincerely set out to follow

Jesus who lived to regret it. I am especially glad, how-ever, that I made the choice to be a Christian in my youth. Because of that early decision, Jesus has not only *cleansed* me from sin, but He has also *kept* me from sin. There is no telling where I would be or what I would be doing were it not for Jesus.

The events leading up to my decision to become a Christian bring to mind an important question, namely, "How did my family and friends help me?" To say it another way, "What can a family do to assist their children in determining to follow Christ?" Perhaps from my experience I can give one answer to this ques-tion.

I was given an atmosphere for it. My home-life provided an environment that was conducive for grow-ing a Christian. We went to Bible class and worship regularly. We attended each night of the gospel meetings that came along, and we were part of any social get-togethers of the church. I was reared *among* the church, you might say. Our home was a place for numerous discussions about the Scriptures. Dad and Mother re-garded the Scriptures as the inspired Word of God, and their belief rubbed off on the children. There was never any question as to whether or not we loved God. We all did, and everyone knew it.

When you think about it, given the right kind of home, it is a natural thing for a child as he moves from childhood to manhood to want to be a Christian. The child has lived his life in the atmosphere, the heavenly air of Christianity. A Christian home teaches the children in it to be Christians by what it is, by its everyday life, by the breath it breathes.

Further, I was taught. Beside Bible classes, there were numerous teaching moments that popped up here and there that helped me along. One such time came while I was alone in the pickup truck with my brother Gene. We were waiting for the bin of the combine to fill with wheat so that we could take the wheat to the barn for storage. My brother, who is nine years older than I am, was driving the truck, and I was riding with him, helping with "the little things."

Gene began the conversation with the simple words "Are you thinking about becoming a Christian?" I answered, "Yes," and he took it from there. Pulling a little New Testament from his shirt pocket, he went over the plan of salvation that is given to us in the Scriptures. I needed that little study. I had my mind pretty much made up, but I needed a little more teaching, a little reassurance, and a little encouragement. He just added strength to the mountain of teaching that I had already received.

Still further, I was encouraged. In the evenings of this particular week, we were going to Springdale for the services of a gospel meeting that was being held. The preacher was the famous G. K. Wallace, a great preacher and a wonderful Christian. As Daddy and I got in the truck that evening to leave for the service, we had just a few minutes alone together before my mother and my sister, Savanna, joined us. They usually came to the truck about five to ten minutes after we did. It took them a little longer to get ready, and I was glad. While we waited, I looked at Daddy and quietly said, "Daddy, tonight I'm going to become a Christian." I doubt that my statement took him by surprise. Surely, he knew I was thinking about it. He said, "Wonderful. Is there any way that I can help you?" I said, "Yes. I want us to sit close to the front. I'm nervous, and I don't want to have far to walk." He said, "We will do just that! We will get close to the front." However, Daddy made a promise that he could not keep. We got to the service a little late, at least too late for the front seats. Can you imagine? Those were the days when gospel meetings were popular, and the buildings were nearly full every night. Nevertheless, we found a pew that was in about the middle part of the auditorium. When all were settled in, I found myself in the middle of the pew, having five or so people to squeeze past on my way to the aisle when I would be responding to the invitation.

I think that was the shortest sermon I have ever heard! Before I knew it, we were standing to sing the invitation song. It was time for me to respond, but I could not move. It was as if my feet were glued to the floor. Instead of allowing myself to talk to me, I quickly started talking to myself. I said, "When we get to this word in the invitational hymn, we are going to move! I mean every part of

my body. We're all going. Does everyone understand?"
We came to that word, and the rest is history. The devil
cannot win over a boy whose mind is made up. As I
started toward the aisle, people moved this way and that
to let me out. I was almost running when I got to the front.

The local preacher, Mac Layton, met me at the front
of the aisle, said "God bless you" to me, and then took me
by the hand and seated me on the front pew. While I sat
and waited for the conclusion of the invitation song—
with lips trembling, eyes batting back tears, my heart
beating rapidly, and I guess with my body shaking all
over—I felt a gentle hand on my shoulder, saying with
just a touch, "God bless you, young man. You have made
the right decision. We will be on the journey with you.
We are standing here behind you, and we are backing you
up all the way." Following my confession of Jesus and
my baptism into Christ for the remission of my sins,
several others came to me and expressed their congratu-
lations and love.

When we buried our dad, I suggested to my siblings
that we place on the grave marker—which would be the
grave marker for both Dad and Mom—the words "In
whom our faith first dwelt." You will recognize this
phrase as coming from 2 Timothy 1:5. Timothy's faith
first dwelt in his grandmother Lois and in his mother
Eunice. Our faith first dwelt in our dad and mother.

I chose this epitaph for a good reason. I meant by it
that our parents, early on, pointed us to the means by

which faith—the same faith they had in the Lord—could be created and maintained in us. True faith can only come through accepting and abiding in the Word of God. Parents cannot give their faith to their children. It is not that easy. No one can borrow someone else's faith; it always springs from the sacred Scriptures. Faith cannot be given away; faith is a personal relationship with Jesus. The written Word brings us to faith in the Living Word, Jesus.

However, parents can provide an atmosphere in which it is natural for their children to want to have faith in Jesus; they can teach their children the Word of the Lord in special, teachable moments in their lives. As their children respond to that Word with trust and love, and as faith becomes a living reality in them, they can put a hand on their shoulders and say, "God bless you. We are here to make the journey with you. We will assist you, and you will assist us."

"It costs a lot to be a Christian,
but it costs a lot more not to be one."

"We either live for Christ
or forever wish we had."

"Jesus built a bridge to God for us
with two beams and three nails."

7

TRUSTING IN TRIBULATION

"These things I have spoken to you, so that in Me you may have peace. In the world you have tribulation, but take courage; I have overcome the world" (John 16:33).

Indeed, all who desire to live godly in Christ Jesus will be persecuted (2 Timothy 3:12).

It does not take a new Christian long to learn that the world around him is no friend of grace to help him along in his walk with God. If the devil cannot keep us from becoming Christians, if he cannot entice us into unfaithfulness after we become Christians, he will do his best to discourage us from living for Christ and render us useless. He will use our circumstances, the people around us, and even weak or unfaithful brethren to dish out disheartening words, put up roadblocks, pour cold water on our spirits, or even lead us headlong into evil. He has an array of weapons in his arsenal, and he uses all of them frequently and effectively.

While on the purest and noblest mission of effecting the redemption of the world, the holy Son of God was attacked by the evil one (Matthew 4:1–10). You would think that One on such an errand of mercy would have no opposition from anyone, but only encouragement and good will from everyone. Not so. Opposition was embodied in the nature of the case. Christ came to bring salvation and to destroy the works of the devil, so opposition was inevitable. Thus, after He was baptized, He was immediately led by the Spirit to a high mountain to do battle with Satan, the bitter enemy of all righteousness. After the Spirit descended in the form of a dove, there came the devil of temptation; after the water came the wilderness. He confronted the Tempter with the testimony of Scripture and defeated him beyond dispute. Someone has said, "If the Lord could defeat the devil with three passages from Deuteronomy, we ought to be able to defeat him with an entire Bible."

As a young Christian with a tender conscience and an eager determination to be what the Lord has asked us to be, it was a rude awakening for me to discover that not everyone was going to be encouraging or would relish the taste of heavenly things. My zeal would sometimes be met with comments like "Don't take this too seriously," and my simple attempt at obedience to the Word would draw the response "Remember, no one is perfect."

Naturally, the place of the fieriest struggles was with my peers at school, in the circle of my closest friends. Sometimes a young person has to make the difficult choice of pleasing his or her friends or pleasing his or her God. He has to decide what is going to come first. It is a big trial for a teen-ager, perhaps the biggest trial. I had turned my face toward Jesus and consequently had resolutely turned my back on evil. I knew I was not faultless, but I was trying to be blameless. Oh, no, I was not perfect. I was far from it, as those who knew me in those days could—and frequently do—testify, but I understood the implications of such a lifestyle. The big positive, following Jesus, would result in many sanctified negatives: activities I could not participate in, books I could not read, and places where I would not be able to go. I knew that there would have to be a forsaking before there could be a filling. It was clear to me that a person full of sin could not be indwelt by the Savior.

I remember the agony I experienced in my early to mid-teen years because of my commitment to be a Christian. My decisions were often poorly made, and sometimes the results were not what I thought they would be; but I was making my decisions from the viewpoint of trying to walk as Jesus had walked. My biggest discouragement was not having around me friends who shared my dream of being a child of God. I had friends, but when I was with them I had to step into another world, a secular world to which I was trying to say goodbye. My friends were good friends, but they were not Christians. They were worldly people. At recess, at noon, and in Physical Education, I was confronted with evil, close up and personal, in the words, thoughts, and conduct of boys my age. They thought it was smart to be sinful. A young boy trying to be a Christian in that group stood out like an elephant among horses, either despised or considered a nonentity. I was not about to give up my commitment, but I became a quiet Christian. I fell into the trap of just being a Christian when in worship or in Bible class. I would not participate in sinful activities, but neither would I openly condemn them. I opted for a peaceful coexistence with the dark things of this world.

I stumbled through those years. By the grace of God and the strength that only Jesus can give, I made it through. The victory is His, not mine. If I had known then what I know now, of course I could have handled those days much better and would have been more fruitful. Hindsight is always better than foresight, and the wisdom of years is always better than the inexperience of youth. Perhaps sharing what I would think about if I were now thirteen to fifteen years of age might encourage some dear heart who is in that age bracket, or it could remind us all of how we might encourage young Christians when we have the opportunity.

I wish I had known that difficulty is part of the package. When I became a Christian, no one explained this part of the Christian life to me. They reminded me of the blessings and the privileges, but they did not make me read the fine print. Jesus faced His cross, and we must face ours. Every day is a cross-bearing day. The Lord in His Word did not promise a smooth, easygoing Christian life. He promised one of conflict with the forces of darkness, one of trials that grow one's faith, and one that sometimes walks the path of truth in loneliness. The road was rocky for the Son of God, and it will be so for every genuine follower of His. The Christian is a soldier doing battle, not the "enjoy this life" type of person who avoids spiritual sweat, strain, and struggle at all costs.

When you think about it, the suffering Christian is part of a great company. Time would fail one to tell of Noah, Moses, Daniel, Peter, Paul, and thousands of others whose footprints have been left behind with drops of blood in them. God takes the furnace of suffering and uses it as an incubator to grow stronger Christians. It takes the friction of a file to sharpen an ax; it takes adversity to refine our faith.

Does all this mean that the joy of Jesus and the gladness of God are, in fact, nonexistent or just pious platitudes with no truth behind them? Perish the thought! The sweet song of the soul that Christ gives will be heard in the thickest battle, in the heart of the lone soldier as he stands against the world with the truth. Heavenly music will be present in the faithful teen-ager who makes a feeble attempt to be a dedicated Christian among a crowd of friends who could not care less about God. Christians can sing in the night when their backs are bleeding and their hands are chained. The beauty of the peace that Christ gives is that it is not dependent upon favorable circumstances. It laughs at adversity. The devil did not give it, and he cannot take it away. The nightingale sings its sweetest in the darkest part of the night, and the peace of Christ is most evident in the heart of a Christian who is facing the darkest trial (see Acts 6:15).

I wish I had been more aware that I was not alone. In the midst of our hardships, it seems as if we are the only ones living for Christ. We tend to say, "I have to be the only one in the world who is facing this trial." No, there are others; you just do not see them at the time.

Very early, I began to dream of a place where there would be dozens of others my age who were seeking to be the Lord's followers. A few years later, I found such a place at a Christian college. However, one would be terribly mistaken to say that a Christian college is the only such place. No, indeed, I have learned to look around. Yogi Berra said, "You see a lot by observing." Look and see. Congregations of the Lord's people comprise that place; the Christian home becomes that place; and, with the proper choosing, our circle of friends becomes that place.

In those early years, I had not learned to choose Christian friends. I had not tapped into the precious fellowship of the church as I should have, and I had not leaned upon the Christian fellowship in my own home as I could have.

I wish I had known or believed more fully that "this too will pass." Trials are only temporary. The day came, as it does for every Christian, when I found Christian friends everywhere who shared the same battles, hopes, dreams, and blessings. I look back now on those teenage hardships and wonder why they were so troublesome to me. Distance makes a difference in the view of course.

Paul said that one day in heaven you will look back on the distress, pressure, and tribulation of this world and declare that they are not even worthy to be compared with the glory that has been bestowed upon the saints (Romans 8:17). One day in the sweet by and by—in the city we can only see now through the eyes of faith, when all our struggles have passed—we will sit down, remember, and rejoice over the victories that the Lord gave us.

Some people in the neighborhood found out that Dad and Mom always went to worship service, without fail, every Sunday morning, Sunday evening, and Wednesday evening. They took note of the time they would be gone, and one Sunday evening while Dad and Mother were gone to worship, they cut the fence and slaughtered a good-sized calf. It was a three-hundred-dollar loss to Dad, a large loss to him at that time. The next morning Daddy found the cut wire, and he could see that a calf had been stolen. The police were called, but the theft was never resolved. This incident, however, as terrible as it was to them, did not affect their going to worship at all. They seemed to be totally undaunted by it. I asked Daddy shortly after it happened, "How do you feel about it?" His answer has stuck with me. He said, "Sometimes, you just have to take it on the chin and go on." He was right, was he not?

Young Christians—and all other Christians—have to remember that in this life we will have tribulation; but we can rejoice in the midst of it, for Jesus has overcome the world. When the trials come, just take them on the chin; with the strength of Jesus and the glory of heaven in your soul, go on. One day, from the portals of glory if not before, you will rejoice over them as you behold the outcome of your faith. You have the Lord's word on it. Jesus turned His crown of thorns into a wreath of eternal victory; He gives each of His disciples the power and the motivation to take life's perils and turn them into pearls of triumph. This world is a place of discipline and training. We are in boot camp, not in paradise valley.

സ്ലോ

"Life is a grindstone: It will either polish you up
or grind you down, depending upon
what you are made of."

"You cannot sharpen an ax on a pound of butter."

8

LIVING AS A FAMILY

God created man in His own image, in the image of God He created him; male and female He created them (Genesis 1:27).

Then the Lord said to Cain, "Where is Abel your brother?" And he said, "I do not know. Am I my brother's keeper?" (Genesis 4:9).

The beginning of the human race and the origin of the human family occurred at the same time. God did not begin one without the other. In His wisdom, He chose to make every human being a member of a family. Consequently, our lives are so intertwined with family living that it is hard for us to imagine what life would be like if we had to live in this world alone, separated from any kind of supportive family. As we think about this question, our minds just go blank. We say to ourselves, "God knew what He was doing when He made the family. Who would want to be a human being apart from a family?"

To help us appreciate our own family ties, let us go back to the beginning of the family and see what God intended for the family. Let us even go back to that special moment before human history when the holy Trinity said,

> Let Us make man in Our image, according to Our likeness . . . (Genesis 1:26).

This council meeting of Deity, if you will, was the beginning of the beginning of the human race, for it suggests the purpose for which the race would be created. After the Godhead announced its resolve for the ages of time, the actual creation took place. The almighty hand of God reached down and scooped up a lump of earth and fashioned it into the physical form of the first man. The body that was created was miraculously, artistically, and wondrously made, but it was vacant; it was an empty house, a lifeless form. Perhaps it was like a mannequin in a clothing store window. Then, wonder of wonders, God breathed into that physical form the energy and vitality of life and combined that life with an eternal spirit, thus making a human being come together in that body. Adam was not a body who had a soul; he was a soul who had a body. His eyes did not see; he saw with his eyes. His ears did not hear; he heard with his ears.

All of the other living creatures of the earth had already been created, and some of them possessed better eyesight than Adam. Some of them had greater physical strength than man, and some of them had better hearing capabilities than man. Nevertheless, man was different and was greater than all of them because he bore the likeness of God; he had the capability of walking with God in divine fellowship.

As Adam stood up and looked around at the world in which God had placed him, God announced that He was giving man dominion over the animals of the forests and fields, the fish of the seas and streams, and the birds of the air. God had not created man for the world; He had created the world for man.

The rulership over all things that God had given man, as Adam would later discover, would involve freedom of choice, or free moral responsibility. God did not want a mindless robot; he wanted a man who could and would recognize, understand, and live by the truth He had revealed to him. However, in order for man to be able to choose what is good, God had to make it possible for man to choose what is evil. In giving man the freedom of choice, God had given him an opportunity to do good and to exercise his noblest capacity, his capacity to choose what is right and true.

God would place man, therefore, under the restraint of His will, and He expected man to acknowledge His will and obey it. God gave man eyes; but if He had not made light, what use could he have made of his eyes? He gave man the capacities of taste, smell, and hearing; but in a world without flavors, odors, or sounds, these gifts would have been useless. In giving Adam commandments to obey, God was giving Adam an opportunity to rise to a new level of moral discernment.

As a demonstration that Adam was in charge of the world that God had made, Adam was given the command to name every living creature. Adam had been created with a language and the ability to think and reason, the capacity to name and to identify.

As Adam began the process of giving designations to the animals, fish, and birds, he made an important observation, one that every human being after him has made at one time or another: He needed a companion in life. Every living thing had a mate of some kind except Adam. He saw nothing among the living creatures that would be a suitable living mate for himself. You have heard the expression "A dog is man's best friend." Yes, we can have friendship with a dog, and many people do; but we cannot have fellowship with a dog. One can only have fellowship where there is true kinship. If you were placed on an island far away from all other human beings, it would not take you long to experience loneliness—the kind that is oppressive, debilitating, and devastating. God allowed Adam to experience loneliness because He wanted Adam to see the need for companionship before He gave him a wife.

Witnessing the emptiness of Adam's heart, the Lord God said,

> It is not good for the man to be alone; I will make him a helper suitable for him (Genesis 2:18).

When God caused Adam to go into a deep sleep, He became the first anesthesiologist, the first group of nurses, and the first surgeon, all rolled into one. From Adam's side God took a rib and "built," as the Hebrew language says, the physical body of the first woman. Her body was different from the man's, a complement to it. God then infused into that body an intellect, including emotions, willpower, and conscience. Then He added a spark of Himself to her makeup, and she became an eternal spirit, just as Adam was. She was equal to man, but she was different. She was the perfect companion for man.

The marriage ceremony was brief, unlike most ceremonies today. There were no songs or speeches, not even an exchanging of vows. Most translations of the Scriptures present this wedding in only six words:

> He . . . brought her to the man (Genesis 2:22).

God was the first Minister to officiate at a wedding, and He was the first Father to give away a bride. The wedding was not the important thing with God; what happened afterwards was going to be the meaning of it.

When Adam saw his wife for the first time, he did not utter the grunts and unintelligible groans of a Neanderthal man. The first recorded words of Adam are poetic:

> This is now bone of my bones,
> And flesh of my flesh;
> She shall be called Woman,
> Because she was taken out of Man
>   (Genesis 2:23).

As a kind of reception following the first wedding, the Holy Spirit pronounced a perpetual blessing upon the marriage estate, emphasizing the essentials for a happy marriage:

> Therefore shall a man leave his father and his mother, and shall cleave unto his wife: and they shall be one flesh (Genesis 2:24; KJV).

The basic family unit, according to the Holy Spirit, rests upon two practical pillars of living: leaving and cleaving. There must be a separation from the former family, and there must be the cleaving of one to the other as the new family is formed. This leaving must become a permanent "leaving," and the cleaving must be a continual "cleaving unto."

Horace William Cloer and Madge Langley, my parents, in harmony with the holy estate of marriage that God has set up, were married February 4, 1928, in Long

Beach, California, and thus my immediate family began. I did not join the family until 1944. When I entered the family, it had six members: Dad and Mother, and four children, Bill, Bob, Gene, and Savanna.

Reflect on the early years of your family living. Think about what you see. As I mention what I see, perhaps you will see similar things.

The family is God's design. We cannot be a part of a good family and not see the wisdom of God behind its existence. For example, every family needs a head and a heart. Daddy was the unquestioned leader of our family, and Mother was the heart. When I wanted to make a big decision, I went to Daddy; when I wanted sympathy, I went to my mother.

All major decisions rested with Daddy. Everyone knew it. No one ever questioned it. This arrangement is the arrangement God intended. Read Ephesians 5:23. Even Shakespeare said, "If two men are going to ride a horse at the same time, someone must ride in front." You cannot have two leaders in the home—if you have two trying to lead, chaos will reign.

There is symbolism in the way God created everything. Why did God create man first and then later create the woman? You answer, as I have already said, "He wanted man to experience loneliness before God gave him a companion." Yes, that is true, but there is another reason: He wanted us to see that He had a different role for the man than He had for the woman.

After Paul had declared that the woman should not have authority over the man, he gave two reasons for announcing this truth, one of which was the order of creation. He said:

> For it was Adam who was first created, and then Eve (1 Timothy 2:13).

His affirmation and illustration show us beyond any doubt that God was teaching us a lesson in His order of creation that is crucial for us to remember and important for us to practice in our homes.

This fact does not mean that the woman is less important than the man; it just means that she has a different function and a different administrative responsibility. When you think about it, we would have it no other way. I saw the wisdom of God's plan in my home, and I hope you saw it in your home.

The family is mankind's delight. Our home was not perfect, but it was a beautiful place to be. We had many happy times together. As I think about our home, I can easily see that God established the home for the enjoyment of man.

Every child in our family was different, possessing different talents, likes, and dislikes; but we got along and enjoyed each other immensely. We had what every child has to have: love, the security of belonging, and the necessities of life. In our home, there were three beautiful companions: love, laughter, and livelihood.

The home should be a place of discipline and learning, but it should also be a place of joy and peace. My heart goes out to any child who lives in a sad, doleful home. May we never take something that God intended to be for man's blessing and turn it into an environment colored with black crepe.

The family is everyone's duty. To have the home that God wants us to have, and to have the home that everyone needs, every member of that home must do his or her part. Read Ephesians 6:1–4. There are times when the whole family has to sacrifice for the one in trouble, and there are times when the wishes of the individual will have to be given up for the needs of the entire family.

Each child must have space to grow, develop, and live his or her own life. Each member of my family was different from everyone else. Bill was an athlete, determined and businesslike; Bob was an outdoorsman, a hunter unparalleled; Gene was a preacher, thoughtful and concerned; Savanna was creative and aspiring, a young woman of great talent. Each was given room to live and grow and to become what he or she wanted to be. However, each was expected to contribute to the soundness, success, and strength of the family.

Adam had his responsibilities toward Eve, and Eve had hers toward him. When children came, Adam and Eve focused on them as well as on each other. The children, though they were different in disposition and aptitude, were to look out for each other. Read Genesis 4:10.

Even though the family is God's design, mankind's delight, and everyone's duty, it has been placed in our hands to do with what we will. God gave the gift, but we must decide what we are going to do with it. He has given us the freedom to choose.

It has been said that the Prince of Wales approached the small cabin of a miner. He respectfully knocked and asked if he could come in. The miner said, "You are my sovereign, and you may come in anytime you wish." "No," said the prince, "your home belongs to you. No one, not even a prince, may enter it without your permission."

The greatest Sovereign has given us control of our homes. We have the responsibility to make the home into what God had in mind for it when He created it. God has said to us, in essence, "I know what you must have, and I made it for you when I created the family; but it will be up to you to build it out of the blueprint I gave you."

You must have some kind of house to have a home, but you can have a nice house, a beautiful mansion, and not have a home. A home is the right kind of family that lives in some kind of a house.

Is there a Christian home in your house?

9

BEGINNING TO PREACH

For we do not preach ourselves but Christ Jesus as Lord, and ourselves as your bond-servants for Jesus' sake (2 Corinthians 4:5).

But we have this treasure in earthen vessels, so that the surpassing greatness of the power will be of God and not from ourselves (2 Corinthians 4:7).

At the age of fifteen, I must admit, I was not a young man of ambition and aspiration. I was characterized by ambivalence and perplexity. I was wandering around without drive or dreams. I knew that I wanted to be a Christian, but I had given little thought to what my profession or occupation in life would be. Perhaps I was a typical fifteen-year-old, living mainly for the present and putting off until another day the big decisions that would mold my future.

One late afternoon, during milking time, in January 1960, my mind was made to think about an ambition for my life. My brother Gene and his wife, Betty, had come from Farmington to visit with us. Betty went into the house to visit with Mother, and Gene came to the dairy barn to visit with Dad and me while we were finishing the evening milking.

Gene began to tell about how the elders of the Farmington church had put him in charge of planning a youth meeting for a Sunday afternoon that was a month away. I became nervous as the conversation proceeded, because I was uneasy about what might come up. Sure enough, what I feared arose: Gene asked if I would give one of the talks at that youth meeting. Two talks would be given, and he wanted me to give one. I was terrified! My mind began to whirl with what giving a talk would be like. I had never given a talk before a congregation of the church before; furthermore, I had never really planned to give one. I was the last person I could picture standing before an assembly giving a message about the Lord. I had found it difficult to lead a public prayer, and now I was being asked to give a short sermon! Just thinking about it caused me to tremble inside, caused my heart to beat rapidly, and made me feel faint. Before I could answer, he pulled from his shirt pocket an outline on the eight Christian graces in 2 Peter 1:5–7 and said, "Here is an outline of the passage that you could speak about. You might even want to follow the arrangement I have put down on the paper."

Gene is nine years older than I am, and we had a mutual admiration for each other, as most brothers do. The mutuality was this: I looked up to him, and he wanted to make something out of me.

Marriage had been good for Gene. He had settled down and was working in the church. He had even preached a sermon or two. He saw possibilities in me that I had not even thought about. He believed that he could turn a weed into a flower—if not into a rose, at least into a lily.

Motivated by my appreciation for Gene, and without thinking much about how I would do it, I did something that is amazing to me to this day: I said that I would give the talk if he would help me with it as much as he could. Little did I realize that his invitation to give that talk was going to be a major turning point in my life! An aimless teen-ager was going to receive some guidance that would remarkably influence what he was going to do with his life.

In the days ahead, I worked conscientiously on what I was going to say. I was not about to walk into that pulpit without having thoroughly planted in my mind what I was going to present. We did not have any books, such as commentaries or Bible dictionaries, at our house. I just had to use what was available: a dictionary in the back of a big Bible, a copy of *Cruden's Concordance*, and some back issues of *The Firm Foundation* that we had kept. I was determined that I would do the best that I could. If I failed, it would not be because I did not try.

One of my evening chores was taking seven or eight bales of hay to the cows after they had been milked. This responsibility gave me an unusual opportunity to go over what I was going to say. As I drove the tractor to the place where the hay would be unloaded for the cows, I would go over my talk—even saying it out loud as I tossed out the hay. The cows heard me, but I do not think anyone else did. I do not think it bothered the cows. (They may have even mooed a gentle "amen" at times, for all I know.) One thing is sure: It helped me a lot. After the chores were done and we were back at the house for the evening, I would take the Bible, the concordance, and the periodicals we had and study as best I could through anything that I was unclear on. I tried to remember every Bible class I had ever been in and every sermon that I had ever heard for additional understanding of the passage I was studying.

As the calendar moved closer and closer toward the day of that youth meeting, I became more and more nervous. It is a wonder that my body and mind withstood all that pressure and strain. I still remember to this day the inner tension and turmoil I felt.

As I recall, I had only worn a suit on two special occasions, Gene's and Savanna's weddings. The only suit I had was a gift from a dear Christian woman whose memory I will cherish until the end of my sojourn on this earth. It was one that her son had outgrown; it was a hand-me-down, but it was like a new one to me. This youth meeting was a suit-wearing event, so we got out my only suit and made sure it was ready to be worn! We found a tie that would go with it, and I began counting down the days.

The youth meeting would not take place until Sunday afternoon at 2:00 o'clock, and young people from all over Northwest Arkansas would be coming. It was a monthly youth gathering that was hosted by a different congregation each month. When Sunday morning came, I was a basket case. I thought I was going to die. I was fairly calm on the outside, but I was a virtual tornado on the inside. My biggest fear was forgetting what I had planned to say. After the Sunday morning service, we came home, we ate a bite, and then I got ready to go to Farmington. My mother and my sister helped me with my tie and my tie tack. Until that day, I thought a tie tack was just for decoration; however, my sister made clear to me that the purpose of a tie tack is to hold the tie in place!

We drove to Farmington and greeted some of the young people who had gathered. Soon the service started. I was seated on the front pew, awaiting my turn to speak. I do not remember who the other speaker was. I just remember that the time for me to speak came quickly. Before I knew it, I was up before about two hundred Christian youths and adults, trying to lead them in a brief study of God's Word. It seemed as if my knees could not even knock—they were missing! I thought I was wobbling, so I took hold of the pulpit and held on for dear life. I thought my lesson might last twenty to twenty-five minutes, but I blazed through it in thirteen minutes flat!

In the midst of the fear, the excitement, and the nervous tension, something wonderful happened to me that afternoon. Out of the darkness of strain and difficulty arose a beautiful light of hope. I began a thrilling journey that day that I have been on ever since. That afternoon, I began to realize that perhaps I could do something for the Lord's cause other than just sit on a pew in a church building. A new joy came into my soul— a joy of believing that I could return something to my Lord for what He had done for me. I knew the Word of God should be taught, and now I was coming to believe that maybe I could teach and preach it.

I do not tell about my beginning to preach on that Sunday afternoon just to relate to you a chapter from my life. I would like to make a point. Let us think back over this episode that I experienced and see if we can identify the key ways to encourage a young man to begin thinking about giving his life to preaching the gospel.

It is obvious that the encouragement should begin with building a fire of respect in his heart. I remember the tremendous respect I had for preachers and their work. This view of preaching had come from my home-life and from the influence of the local congregation of which we were a part. Everything I had heard about preachers, everything I had seen preachers do and say, and all that the Springdale congregation had taught me about preaching and preachers had influenced me. My parents and the brethren did not know it, but through the years—with their attitudes and their other types of examples—they were instilling in my young mind an appreciation for full-time ministers of the Word that would be the mental environment in which a flame for preaching could be ignited. A match cannot set rocks afire! A flame of sacred love can only bring to a blaze the spiritual kindling wood that is stored up in the heart.

I had been taught by what I had heard and seen that preaching was the highest enterprise in which anyone could engage. I had come to understand that preaching is the way a righteous man co-labors with God in building the church and in creating new Christians. Until young men have the proper appreciation for the wonderful task of preaching, their minds will not be the fertile fields for the spark of inspiration to challenge them to preach the Word.

This encouragement should include giving them reasonable guidance at the beginning. A young man needs more than just the words "Why don't you make a talk?" Some instruction should be given to him. It may have to be given in subtle ways. We cannot build the lesson for the young man, but we can provide basic assistance that will steer him in the right direction. Young men are not born with the ability to outline a lesson from God's Word, and a little help on this topic will go a long way. Had Gene not given me a short outline, I do not know what I would have done.

The encouragement should include giving him time to prepare. We may not see making a talk as a big step for a young man, but most likely he does. He should be given perhaps two or three weeks to put his lesson together. If he does not realize the importance of the time needed for preparation, he should be made to see the importance of it. James said that few should be teachers because of the responsibility that goes with it (James 3:1). We are not doing him a favor by rushing him into the pulpit before he has had time to think seriously, plan carefully, and pray fervently about what he will teach.

The encouragement we give him should be meaningful and realistic. It does not help to tell him that he is going to be the greatest preacher who has ever lived. A young man does not know yet to "smell the flowers but not swallow them." We need to let him know the facts in the case: He can be a good preacher if he continues to work, grow, and prepare. It is important to be realistic and not ridiculously idealistic.

Following my first little talk, my friends and loved ones were kind and considerate; they spoke thoughtfully to me. They knew what I had been through, and they appreciated me for toughing it out. They did not rush up to me gushing with praise, but they were eager to give me practical encouragement.

The encouragement should include giving him other opportunities. One learns to preach by preaching, just as one learns to sing by singing. Of course, receiving only one opportunity to make a talk will not be sufficient to encourage a young man to grow into a preacher.

Two or three weeks after this first talk, an opportunity came from one of the elders at the Springdale congregation for me to give another talk, this time on Wednesday night. Through my brother-in-law's influence, I soon received an opportunity to preach a full-length sermon. I needed additional opportunities, but I could not provide them myself; I had to have help.

We should encourage him by sharing our wisdom with him. At opportune times he needs older men in the faith to share with him the wisdom that they have gleaned through the years on how to live the Christian life and how to do the work of the church. An older preacher needs to take him under his wing.

When I would see them at the gas station, in the grocery store, or at leisure times, dear, godly men would talk with me about what they knew about preaching. I remember those times and treasure them as important times of learning and growing.

Encouraging a young man to preach is a community/ church project. It requires the home, the local church, and the churches in a region. It is a united effort. Everyone in Christ should adopt him, taking advantage of any opportunity to inspire him, to cultivate him, or to provide opportunities for him to grow into a preacher of the everlasting gospel. After all, what greater thing can we do than to encourage one to become a preacher?

"Don't go out and preach unless you preach as you go out."

—*Augustine*

"There is no greater need on earth than that of raising up quickly faithful gospel preachers and teachers worldwide."

10

MY HOME CONGREGATION

. . . And the Lord was adding to their number day by day those who were being saved (Acts 2:47).

And He put all things in subjection under His feet, and gave Him as head over all things to the church, which is His body, the fullness of Him who fills all in all (Ephesians 1:22, 23).

God has created only three institutions: the home, the civil government, and the church.

The home was created first, for it was part of the package that came with the human race. God set it up so that every person would be a part of some kind of a family.

The civil government came next. We can easily see how that civil government became a necessity as the population of the earth grew. The Book of Judges confirms that when "everyone does what is right in his own eyes," confusion and anarchy will fill the land. Law is required for the orderliness of society. God provided for this need of the human race by giving us the principle of government. In the Scriptures, the permanent establishment of the exercise of government was announced shortly after Noah came out of the ark.

> "Surely I will require your lifeblood; from every beast I will require it. And from every man, from every man's brother I will require the life of man. Whoever sheds man's blood, by man his blood shall be shed, for in the image of God He made man" (Genesis 9:5, 6).

Man has not always executed the principle of government properly or with the total interests of the people in mind. Nevertheless, God has urged His people to be submissive to the civil powers under which they live (Romans 13:1–7).

The church was created third. It was established through Jesus—by His earthly ministry, by His death and resurrection, and by the preaching of His gospel on the Day of Pentecost. Its coming was the fulfillment of the eternal purpose that God set in motion at the beginning of time.

The church can be defined as people who at the time of their obedience to Christ's gospel are welded into a community or family by the Spirit. This community of obedient believers is the spiritual body of Christ that worships God and does His work in this world. Jesus said He was going to build this community, and He called it His church (Matthew 16:18).

In New Testament times, one was added to this body by the gracious hand of God (Acts 2:47). A person could not "join" His church. Membership in it could only result from one coming to Jesus on the terms of His gospel and Jesus saving him through His blood.

No denominations existed in those days. Man had not been able to clutter up the religious scene with his man-made institutions, which secular wisdom deemed more suitable for man than the institution Jesus had ordained. Those first years of Christianity were times of pure Christianity. The early Christians were under the guidance of inspired men, and they were being led to be the kind of Christians God had always intended for man to be. They were submissive and obedient to the leadership of the Spirit of God that was given to them through inspired men.

The act of becoming a Christian constituted the same act as becoming a member of the body of Christ, the church. God did not set up a Christless church, nor did He send a churchless Christ. The result of Jesus' earthly ministry was the church. Whoever belonged to Christ belonged to His church.

Dad and Mother became Christians in 1936, and my brothers and sister followed, with Bill becoming a Christian in 1940, Gene in 1947, Savanna in 1952, and me in 1955. Then, in 1964, I was privileged to baptize Bob one afternoon in White River. We wanted to belong to Christ and His church. Desiring to live by the Scriptures that God gave, we sought to follow the Bible as our only religious creed. We aspired to be just Christians in all of the glorious implications of that word.

One of the incredible blessings that I enjoyed as I grew up was that of being a part of a wonderful congregation of New Testament Christians. As I think of the way God has encouraged us and led us, I have to mention the South Thompson Street church of Christ as being a paramount blessing that He gave us. My heart sinks into sorrow when I think of families who have not had the joy and benefit of being a part of a faithful congregation of the Lord's people while they were rearing their children.

Why was this church such a blessing in my life?

It was a church that gave us solid and effective preaching. Every family needs to hear good preaching. The elders, deacons, and members believed in preaching that was true to the Word of God and effectively presented. They saw to it that the regular preaching was of the highest caliber. The sermons were biblical, well organized, and persuasive. They were lovingly delivered and joyfully received.

Perhaps twice a year, the church brought in the finest preachers for the gospel meetings that we would have.

The brethren rejoiced over these exceptional opportunities for hearing God's Word expounded. There was no emotionalism, no appealing just to the emotions; rather, there was a seeking to bring to God our purest intellects, with genuine love, clear consciences, and resolute will. We knew that there is no devotion without emotion, but that there is no real faith without intellectually accepting the evidence of God and acting upon it.

This attitude toward preaching produced in all of us a respect for faithful preachers and preaching. The brethren did not believe in sermonettes; they wanted strong, scriptural, detailed sermons that brought before the congregation the will of God.

It was a church that provided thrilling and faithful teaching. For the most part, the classes we had were a joy to attend and not just something to endure. Usually the teachers were well prepared and manifested a depth of spirituality that would put many church leaders to shame.

How blessed a young man is to be able each Sunday to visit with and grow up around great spiritual giants, men of faith and wisdom. The men I knew did not have any formal schooling in a Christian college, but they knew God, walked with Him, and trusted in His Word. They lived with His Word—and it showed in their faces, in their commitment to good works, in their demeanor, and in their faithful support of gospel preaching.

It was a church that emphasized personal evange-

lism. The Jule Miller Filmstrips had come out by that time, and some of the men of the church were using them. Several of the men of the church had become powerful personal evangelists. Calvin White one day asked me if I wanted to go with him to a cottage meeting. Frankly, I did not know what a cottage meeting was, but I had heard the expression used and wanted to know more about it. I eagerly went. We studied through the filmstrips with a good man, and eventually we were privileged to see him become a Christian. I was quickly convinced that personal evangelism should be a vital part of the work of the church.

It was a church that believed in prayer. Often the elders would pray on their knees after discussing the needs of the church. I will always remember the privilege of praying with them on bended knee. Prayer was not a routine with them; it was their route to strength and wisdom. Prayer was not their final resort; they tried to make it their first resort. They did not believe in prayer, as Charles Hodge says; they believed in God, and they wanted Him to bless them.

It was a church whose members manifested spiritual and Christlike living. There were a few who were not everything they should have been; but, for the most part, the members were serious about living daily for Jesus. They wanted to be Christ's followers. I have heard the excuse "Oh, there are hypocrites in the church. That's why I am not a Christian." Yes, there are hypocrites in the church. There have always been hypocrites. Jesus had Judas; Paul had Demas. Noah, I guess, had to take a skunk on the ark! However, I do not remember meeting many people who were out-and-out hypocrites. The Christians I knew, in the main, were sincerely trying to be Christians, so far as I could tell. They made mistakes, but the mistakes were not intended. Their mistakes were like a train wreck—not scheduled. I never raised the excuse of hypocrites in the church for not being a better Christian; it seems that I was always thinking, "Oh, I wish I could grow up to be a Christian like him!"

It was a church that exhibited compassion for the poor and a love for the lost. They had a genuine concern for preaching the gospel in the other countries of the world. Missionaries often came by and were allowed to speak to us. They gave us a vision that we needed. The elders did not shield us from the appeals of missionaries; they wanted us to hear them. They knew that no church is made poorer when it gives to missionaries.

It was a church that had an appreciation and respect for Christian literature. Occasionally, the members would be encouraged to read well-written tracts and books that would help them to be strong in the Lord. Once Mac Layton announced that several new books had come off the press containing gospel sermons. I signed up for one, and how I enjoyed that book! It was by George W. Bailey, and I literally devoured it. After all these years, I still have it.

We had kept old issues of *The Firm Foundation*. I did not know where we got them. I am sure some of them were given to us. I believe some of them came from a subscription or two that we took when the church was making a list of subscribers for the paper. The elders would urge the members to make sure that gospel litera- ture was coming into their homes. They believed that every Christian should read his Bible and should read good gospel literature.

It was a church that experienced beautiful and mean- ingful fellowship. We enjoyed being together. Eating together and going places together were times of great joy. Our homes were used as the locations for happy get-togethers. The preacher and others would often have all the young people over for an evening of visiting, games, singing, and praying. How we relished those evenings!

It was a church that thanked, praised, and worshiped God. The worship service focused on God, not man. It was a time to say, "Thank You, God, for the blessings You have given." We praised and thanked Him for what He had done for us, and we worshiped Him for who He is. We did not try to slap Him on the back with coarse familiarity; we approached Him with reverence and awe. We saw Him as a compassionate Father toward His people, but we recognized Him as a consuming fire toward sinners outside of His grace.

Think about this church, my home congregation. The

church growth specialists may make spiritual growth in a local congregation too complicated with their statistics, demographics, and charts. When a church has the key traits that I saw and experienced in my home congregation, it will surely grow, even as my home congregation grew. Let us major in curing the disease—and when we do, the symptoms will disappear. When we remove the spider, the cobwebs will no longer plague us. When we turn off the faucet, we will no longer have to mop up the water.

If the church is on the decline where you are, perhaps the eldership could say, "We will look at our preaching, our classes, our personal work, our compassion for the poor and the lost, our use of gospel literature, our fellowship, our prayer life, and our worship services. When we find weaknesses in the light of the Scriptures, we will shore them up." These are the major areas of the life of the church. If we see that we are not strong in any of these areas, we know where we need to place our emphasis for improvement.

No church is going to be perfect, for the church is made of human beings who will be at all the various points on the maturity chart. The congregation at times will level out, with all growing properly and with peace and contentment dropping in for a spell—but that will change, for the evangelism of the local church will bring in more new Christians who will require special care and guidance in the Lord's grace and knowledge.

The church is not a museum of saints; it is a hospital for sinners who have become saints and must be nurtured into health and Christlikeness. We will never have complete and full maturity in the church, and the mature ones will always have the task of kindly leading the weaker ones into a fuller walk with Christ. They should not see their responsibility as a burden, but as a joy similar to the joy a father and mother experience in leading their children into adulthood.

In meeting the needs that appear in the life of the church, I would recommend a response of grace coupled with truth. For example, let us not react to a weakness in preaching in the way suggested by this adage: "If your preacher is not fired up with enthusiasm, fire him enthusiastically." However, it would be in order for the elders to place before the preacher the clear challenge to preach in faith, truth, and love. Sometimes he should preach on what the members want to hear, but most of the time he should say what the members *need* to hear. With this guidance, he will most likely improve, and the congregation will be blessed. If our emphasis is only on truth, we will probably be too severe; but if our emphasis is only on love, we will probably be too sentimental. Emphasizing both brings the true blending of grace and truth that God intended.

I was convinced a long time ago, by the congregation of which I was a part when I was growing up, that any church that wants to grow can grow. Not only can it grow, but it can also become a vibrant congregation of the Lord's church—yes, all this can happen even today!

"Forty-eight percent of the New Testament is about Christ's earthly life, and fifty-two percent of the New Testament is about Christ's church."

"How can one love the Head without appreciating the body?"

"When not much Christianity is seen during the week, don't expect a lot of it to be seen on Sunday."

11

A TEENAGE PREACHER

Let no one look down on your youthfulness, but rather in speech, conduct, love, faith and purity, show yourself an example of those who believe (1 Timothy 4:12).

And He said to them, "Go into all the world and preach the gospel to all creation" (Mark 16:15).

Two twin-like verses in the Old Testament should be pondered carefully and prayerfully by every Christian. These two verses present contrasting views regarding the desires of our hearts.

The first verse is about *the sinful idols of our hearts*. God rebuked the people of Israel concerning the idols that they held secretly in their souls and said that He would answer them according to the idols in their hearts:

> Any man of the house of Israel who sets up his *idols in his heart*, puts right before his face the stumbling block of his iniquity, and then comes to the prophet, I the Lord will be brought to give him an answer in the matter in view of the multitude of his idols, in order to lay hold of the hearts of the house of Israel who are estranged from Me through all their idols (Ezekiel 14:4, 5; emphasis mine).

God said that He would turn Israel over to their sins that they might be punished by them, and perhaps—when they were in the throes of experiencing that anguish—they would return to Him. Their suffering from their sins, God hoped, would drive them to Him in repentance. In eternity man will be punished *for* his sins, but sometimes, as was the case with Israel in this passage, he is punished in this life *by* his sins.

If we persistently seek unholy goals or an ungodly style of living, God will eventually answer us according to the evil we treasure in our hearts. He will let us go to what lures us most. He will allow us to accept what we find most attractive. One way that He may give us this answer is through the natural course of things. Life is so constructed that one generally gets what he or she really wants and earnestly pursues.

For example, God gave this type of answer to Balaam in the Old Testament. Balaam pursued sin and greed until he found himself at the place where his heart had already been for a long time. God let him catch up with his ambition. Balaam was given what he sought most of all, even though it brought about his ruin. While pursuing his dream, he was killed during Israel's battle with the Moabites.

The second verse speaks to *the sacred interests of our hearts*. God gave the beautiful promise that He would answer His children according to the righteous aspirations of their hearts! David wrote:

> Delight yourself in the Lord;
> And He will give you the desires of your heart
> (Psalm 37:4).

Obviously, this promise assumes that the one praying is in tune with God's will and is seeking His righteousness and His authentic will. The qualification is "delight yourself in the Lord." God will grant the desires of the hearts of His people, for He knows their desires will be in line with His will.

Is it not a thrilling thought that God will give us the desires of our hearts if our hearts are sincere and we are desiring the things that are appropriate for God's people to desire? I want you to recount how this has happened in your life, as I relate how it perhaps has happened in mine.

I believe that God answered me according to the desires of my heart when I began preaching. After my first talk on the Scriptures at Farmington, Arkansas, a flame of sacred love was ignited in my heart to preach. It was a small flame at first; however, even as small as it was, it flickered and burned in my innermost being. With time, it grew into a much larger flame.

Maybe a month after my first talk, I was asked to give another talk at Springdale, Arkansas, on a Wednesday night. I do not remember the topic. I just remember that I spoke. After that talk, the flame to preach grew bigger in my soul. Other invitations to give talks came, so I immersed myself in building gospel lessons. I was stumbling along, doing the best I could, craving a better understanding of the Scriptures so that I could preach its glorious message more effectively. In this struggle, a new life was beginning to dawn for me. It was hard for me to do my school work, for I was always secretly thinking about what I was going to preach next instead of thinking about the lesson of the hour.

My brother-in-law, Johnny McCain, was preaching every other Sunday at a small congregation in Forum, Arkansas, about thirty miles from our home. He was helping this small congregation by preaching some for them, but he did not see himself as a preacher of the gospel and did not plan to continue preaching.

One day as we sat around our wood-burning stove in the living room, Johnny asked if I would like to build a full-length sermon and preach it at Forum. If I wanted to do it, he said, he would call the brethren and see if I could preach the next time in his place. I was eager to preach, but I knew that building a complete sermon would be a challenge for me. However, without weighing the responsibility very much, I told him that I would try my best to do it. He gave me about a week and a half to prepare the lesson and promised that he would take me to Forum and introduce me to the brethren.

With my commitment made and with the preaching appointment scheduled, important preparation time lay ahead. I immediately picked out a simple topic and began putting together a sermon on it. The topic was "Let Us Be Constant," and the major points were going to be "in worship," "in Bible study," "in prayer," and "in living for Christ." I put it together and went over it numerous times. Every afternoon when I took the hay to the cows, I preached that sermon from top to bottom. I even extended the invitation. I was going to be ready when the hour to preach came.

Time zoomed by, and the Sunday came. Johnny and Savanna took me to Forum. I had never visited with these brethren before, and I did not know anyone who was a member of that congregation. I was truly a visitor. At the appropriate time, I was introduced, and I walked behind the big pulpit and preached the lesson I had prepared. The congregation was about thirty to forty members in size. They were country folks, with a warm sympathy and a sincere love for a young man who was trying to preach. They listened patiently to my sermon, kindly overlooking my mistakes, and tried to encourage me afterwards.

To my amazement, one of the men, brother Nelson,

came to me after the service and asked if I would be willing to come back to Forum and preach every other Sunday. I said, "What about Johnny? I do not want to interfere with his coming to preach for you." Brother Nelson said, "He has just resigned. He said that he did not want to come anymore and that the church should ask you to come!" With fear and trembling, I told him that I would do my best to come every other Sunday.

It became clear to me that Johnny had planned every detail of this situation. He thought, "If I can get him started at Forum, I will politely bow out. He will have regular preaching opportunities through which he can grow into a preacher." Johnny had been a true brother to his brother-in-law!

A special relationship developed with the Forum congregation. I went to Forum every other Sunday for a while, and then an amazing thing happened: The brother who was coming to Forum the other two Sundays of the month had to resign. In God's good grace, I was asked to do the Sunday morning preaching every week. I accepted their invitation and continued with them through my senior year of high school—a total of two years.

These were challenging days for a teenage preacher who had very little preparation for preaching and a very small library with which to work. When I was first asked to come every Sunday, I did not even have my license to drive. As you can see, I was in over my head in many ways, but I knew that this was a challenge that a young man who was desirous of preaching the gospel should accept.

I have heard about a young man who was preaching his first sermon. He made it through the sermon somehow, but afterwards someone was overheard to say of the sermon, "For the first five minutes, he waded out into water over his head, and for the next twenty-five minutes, he just stood there and blubbered!" I am sure that description would be an apt one for some of my preaching at Forum.

The brethren were patient and encouraging, and I believe that some good was done. God may choose to reveal to us on the other side what was actually accomplished during those days.

Using this early preaching that I did as a backdrop, and relying heavily upon the Scriptures, let us consider what one should do when he is in over his head. It is a fact that often life brings challenges that are too big for us. What should we do with those challenges? How should we handle them?

First, let us remember that dreaming is good. Aspiring to do greater things for the Lord's cause is appropriate for the Lord's people, young and old. A motivation that is driven by a desire for the Lord's cause to prosper and spread will always grow out of the spirit of Christ. It is surely appropriate to aspire to do good works in Jesus' name.

If the challenges are in harmony with God's will and

in line with the direction we believe we ought to go, then let us take them on with fear and trembling. Humility is in order. The task will be achieved with faith, not with arrogance and pride. God will be with us—by strengthening us and by giving us the energy and wisdom to tackle the task. We will do it in His divine power, not in our own.

Let us do the best we can with what we have. God does not ask a five-gallon bucket to carry ten gallons of water. With God's help, we can do far more than we ever thought we could, but there is a sense in which we cannot beat our best.

Let us prepare thoroughly as we seize our opportunities. Preparation is a wonderful key for opening the door to the challenges of life. Moses was prepared for eighty years for forty years of work; John the immerser was prepared for thirty years for maybe six months of preaching; Jesus spent thirty years getting ready for three and one-half years of an earthly ministry. Our God has never instructed us to go out into His service unprepared. His work is extremely important, and He wants His Word to be handled responsibly. Taking time to sharpen the ax is not wasted time, if one is serious about cutting wood.

Let us pray for God to stand with us. Preachers are co-laborers with God. Of course, God has the bigger part in the work, but He expects His servants to hold up their end of the enterprise. We plant and water, but He gives the increase.

Armed with preparation and prayer, let us face opportunities head on. Goliath had to be confronted (1 Samuel 17). David had been prepared for facing him by defending his sheep on the hillsides. He went before Goliath in the name of the Lord, not in his own name. He gathered his five smooth stones and ran straight toward Goliath. He stood before him, looked him in the eye, and put him to sleep with a sedative named "a between-the-eyes stone."

Let us remember that some challenges must be met day by day. There are challenges that come as "one event in time." We deal with such challenges, and then we move on. Some challenges come as stages in our lives that must be faced over a brief period of time; however, others will perhaps have to be faced over a long period of time. In the case of the longer challenges, we must consistently apply these principles as a Christian lifestyle. Persistent faithfulness in these situations is the need.

Let us remember that what we are doing now may be preparation for what God wants us to do later. Those little talks that I gave led the way for bigger opportunities to preach. Had I not given them, I would not have had the courage to accept the bigger challenges.

Let us tackle the God-sent challenges! Life is a place for growth, for rising to the opportunities of service that come, for manifesting faith, and for preparation for the work that God has asked us to do. My preaching at Forum was far from what I wanted it to be, but I did my best at that time with what I had.

I do not pray anymore, "Lord, use me in Your service." I see the value of that prayer, but I do not pray it now. I believe there is a better prayer for a Christian to pray. That is the prayer "Lord, make me usable." The Lord will use anyone who is usable. If we are ready and prepared, God will put us into His service.

God intended for all of us to be workers, not shirkers—servants, not cynics. He wants us on the front lines of the battle, fighting the good fight with faith, diligent in His service, relying on Him for our strength, and determined to be faithful to the One who has saved us.

When we come to the end of life's journey, may it be that all of us can say with Paul to some degree, "I have been faithful to the truth, faithful in the trials, and faithful to the end of the trail—faithful to the faith, to the fight, to the finish." May these words of Paul become your sentiments in your last hour:

> I have fought the good fight, I have finished the course, I have kept the faith; in the future there is laid up for me the crown of righteousness, which the Lord, the righteous Judge, will award to me on that day; and not only to me, but also to all who have loved His appearing (2 Timothy 4:7, 8).

∞

*"Every heart with Christ is a missionary;
every heart without Christ is a mission field."*

*"Do what you can, with what you have,
where you are."*

*"If you wish to be a certain type of person,
assume you are that type of person and then live
out that assumption."*

*"People may doubt what you say, but they
will believe what you do."*

12

NINE DAYS OF GRACE

"Go therefore and make disciples of all the nations, baptizing them in the name of the Father and the Son and the Holy Spirit, teaching them to observe all that I commanded you; and lo, I am with you always, even to the end of the age" (Matthew 28:19, 20).

For since in the wisdom of God the world through its wisdom did not come to know God, God was well-pleased through the foolishness of the message preached to save those who believe (1 Corinthians 1:21).

One of God's ways to comfort His people is through His people who have been comforted. Paul said that God had comforted him; consequently, he was able to share the comfort he had received with others who were in need of the same comfort (2 Corinthians 1:3–6). God's comfort flowed from His great hand of grace through Paul to others.

As a young preacher, I needed both encouragement and comfort, because growing into a gospel preacher had its times of struggle and even its times of frustration. Some brethren thought I was too young to preach, others thought that I did not have the talent to preach, and some brethren did not care whether or not we had any more preachers.

Along the way, however, I ran into brethren who saw the need for raising up preachers, and they believed that almost any young man—even a fellow like me—could be a preacher. They did not look at what is and ask, "Why?" They looked at what could be and asked, "Why not?" From them I received important reassurance and optimism. They wanted me to grow and mature as a preacher of the gospel. With beautiful vision, they sought to open doors of opportunity for growth that would season and strengthen me. These brethren stepped forward and saw that I got what I needed.

For example, in the spring of 1962, the Springdale elders made arrangements with the Evergreen church— a little church that met four or five miles from our home—for me to preach in a gospel meeting that Evergreen wanted to have in July of that year. The Springdale church said that they would provide the financial support for the meeting, while the Evergreen church said that they would host the event by providing the place for the meeting. The Springdale church could not have the meeting, but they could support it; the Evergreen church wanted a meeting, but they could not fund it. They did not have much in their treasury. They had just moved their building, and that expense had depleted their funds.

Thus a gospel meeting was planned. It was to be a two-Sunday meeting. It would be eight days in length and twelve sermons in strength—eight days long and twelve sermons strong.

Elisha Cloer, a brother in Christ and one of our distant relatives, would make the on-site preparations for the meeting since he was a leading member of the Evergreen church. He and I would work closely together as the plans were being formulated.

The little Evergreen church had just moved its building from a location on a dirt road near the river to an attractive site beside Highway 62. The building was small and would hold perhaps forty people if every seat was filled, but it was big enough for the size of the congregation that they were at that time. The only seats they had were old school seats that they had gotten from a school that was being refurbished. However, just before the meeting, through some donations that had come in, they acquired some inexpensive pews. Consequently, this little congregation of Christians was exceedingly thankful for the new location of their building and for the new pews. They were ready to meet and ready to work. It was a good time for them to use their building for evangelism. It would be their first gospel meeting in their new place by the highway, and excitement was in the air. Newness was the word; both the congregation and the preacher were experiencing a beginning. It was sort of a new life for the church, and it was my first gospel meeting!

The meeting was scheduled for the second week of July. However, when Elisha took the flyer that had been designed for advertising the meeting to be printed, a mistake was made: The printing office printed the wrong date. According to the flyer, the meeting would begin on Sunday, go through the next Sunday, and end Monday night. Thus, instead of having an eight-night meeting, the flyer said that we were having a nine-night meeting—a rare type of meeting even in that day. Elisha was concerned about the mistake, but I told him that I had one more sermon and we could go through Monday night if the church agreed to it. He concurred, so we asked a few of the brethren, and they thought it would be best to go through Monday night as well. Therefore, the meeting was set by default to be nine days in length.

I shall never forget that second week of July during the summer of 1962, the week of my first gospel meeting. I have called that meeting "nine days of grace"—for grace was certainly bestowed upon me, and I hope grace was extended to others through the preaching. Events like that meeting just never leave your memory. I can vividly recall all the events that surrounded it, and I can

see myself standing up preaching in the services them-
selves, as if all of these things happened only yesterday.

I worked diligently on the lessons I would present. I
was determined to be ready. When the meeting time
came, I had thirteen sermons in my head and heart—and
they were crying out for me to preach them.

Through the kindness and support of my brethren,
and certainly through the wonderful providence of God,
the little building was packed on the first Sunday night of
the meeting. In fact, some of the people who came could
not get a seat inside the building and had to stand or sit
outside on the steps. This large attendance surprised us
all, but the brethren came up with a simple solution
for the next night. They decided that they would move
the meeting outside for the remaining part of the week.
They put up two poles so that they could string one row
of lights on them and moved their new pews outside,
placing them in a semicircle in front of the building.
I was to use the top part of the steps in the front of the
building as the platform from which to preach. There was
enough room for their pulpit to be placed on that small
space at the top of the steps.

The Evergreen congregation was small in size but
large in spirit. The members were loved by everyone
who knew them. Brethren and friends from miles around
came to encourage them. In addition, some of our friends
and loved ones came to encourage a young preacher
beginning to preach. Thus the attendance was good all

the way through, with perhaps fifty to sixty being present each night. Although that number does not sound like a big attendance now, it was a multitude for us then.

As I remember, some of the topics I preached on were "Can We Understand the Bible Alike?"; "What Must I Do To Be Saved?"; "The Conversion of Saul"; "The Church Jesus Built"; "Why Become a Christian?"; "The Great Judgment Day"; "If I Were the Devil's Preacher"; and "A Plea for Christ."

Westwood Ferguson from the Habberton congregation led the singing, and everyone seemed to enjoy singing outside in the open air. The highway was nearby, and it was a wonder that anybody could hear me over the roar of the traffic; but I did not hear any complaints about the noise. I preached, and those who had gathered seemed to listen.

From Sunday to Sunday, there were no responses to the invitation during the services. Friends, neighbors, and relatives who were not Christians came, but no one made a public response to the invitation. The brethren anticipated that the attendance would be smaller on Sunday morning since the visitors we had with us during the week would go back and worship at their home congregations. Furthermore, since only one more service remained after Sunday, they decided they would have the Sunday and Monday night services inside as well.

When that final Monday night came—the service that only took place because a mistake had been made on the flyers—something memorable happened. For that last service, the little building was completely filled. Seats were brought in from the classrooms to provide additional seating. As I remember, when all the seats were put down, there was no aisle left. Anyone who wanted to respond to the invitation would have to wind around pews and people to get to the front.

After the singing, I preached my sermon, and extended the invitation. I noticed that a friend of ours in the assembly, Everett Johnson, looked nervous. He had come several nights to the meeting, but he was not a Christian. All of a sudden, he left his seat and started toward the front of the auditorium. Going this direction and that, he managed to find a path. Around the pews, through the people, he came to the front and over to me. I took him by the hand and congratulated him on his responding to the gospel. With trembling lips, he said that he wanted to become a Christian. The little church building had no baptistery in it, so we took him to Springdale to baptize him into Christ. What a climax this was to the meeting! Over the years, I have often rejoiced that we continued the meeting through Monday night!

As my first meeting ended, we believed that God had especially watched over what we had tried to do in the name of Christ. After all, we had seen good attendance, we had enjoyed the excitement of open-air worship, and we had been privileged to witness one man, a longtime friend of our family, become a Christian. Now, with forty years of preaching behind me, I have held maybe 850 meetings since then—but I do not think I have ever held one that was any more exciting than that one.

This first meeting teaches us important lessons about life and service to God that I hope we will never forget.

This little meeting reminds us that we need each other. The meeting would never have come about had it not been for the Springdale elders securing for me an opportunity to preach in a meeting. They saw a need, and they took the lead in filling it. I could not have done for myself what they did for me. They did what only elders can do. The precious Evergreen church extended the right hand of fellowship to me and treated me with dignity, honor, and respect, even though I was just a young and inexperienced preacher of the gospel.

You probably can think of people around you who have made it possible for you to have opportunities for growth. You may recognize that those opportunities would never have come to you if not for them. They saw the need and, with genuine concern for you, acted with grace to meet the need. Perhaps you have opened doors for others who otherwise would never have reached the plateau on which they now serve.

The meeting teaches us that unity is a beautiful thing. Here were two congregations—one rather large and the other a small, country one—working together with mutual respect and love, putting together a plan that would encourage a young preacher and save a soul.

Nothing in this world outshines the radiance of brethren united in heart and soul, doing the work of the church. T. B. Larimore—referring to the statement in Psalm 133:1 that unity is both good and pleasant—said that some things are good but not pleasant, like going to the dentist, and that some things are pleasant but not good, like eating candy. However, unity, he said, has both traits: It is at once good and pleasant.

There are three aspects to the unity that we are to have in Christ: an intrinsic unity, a doctrinal unity, and a practical unity. When we enter the body of Christ, the Holy Spirit gives us the intrinsic unity through the blood of Christ. As we stand on the plain teachings of the Scriptures, we enjoy the doctrinal unity. However, only as we work with one another in the give-and-take of daily service do we share and manifest the practical unity that should characterize the church of Christ worldwide.

In that meeting I was taught that the power is in the gospel. God intended for His gospel to be preached to others (Mark 16:15). In every age of human history, He has made His message known through preaching. When an assembly comes together for the purpose of hearing the ancient, everlasting gospel proclaimed, even though most in the assembly have heard it numerous times more effectively presented, something divinely wonderful is taking place. A young preacher doing his best in preaching the gospel can be powerful and helpful, not because of any talent he may or may not have, but because the gospel has given power and importance to what he is doing.

Preaching helps both the preacher and the ones who hear the preacher because of the nature of what preaching is. Preaching is more than a public speech about spiritual things. God uses preaching to draw people to Himself. I know that I was benefited as much or more than those who heard the messages, but I also know that those who heard were blessed as they meditated on His Word, for there is something about the Word of God that is living and active (Hebrews 4:12).

Preaching and fellowship go together. People came early to the meeting and visited with one another; after the service they stayed for further fellowship. In those days, people had time to visit with one another. It is important for a physical family to come together for fellowship, and it is equally important—if not more important—for the family of God to come together to enjoy one another.

This meeting reminded me of the importance of timing. What we view as a mistake may not in actuality be a mistake. It may be only a change of plans. God could even be changing the plans! The meeting seemed to be Everett Johnson's time to make a decision about his soul. Perhaps Everett Johnson would have obeyed the gospel the next Wednesday or the next Sunday, but we cannot be sure. I do know that later on that year Everett died. The meeting, therefore, was a kind of "last opportunity" for him.

Wes Tucker, a great Christian man whom I have known for years, asked me one time, "Tell me about gospel meetings. I do not understand them. Tell me how they work." I said, "Wes, a gospel meeting is like a combine. You do not take a combine out and run over a dusty field where nothing has been planted and nothing is ripe for harvesting. A gospel meeting is a combine that you bring in to harvest the golden grain of souls." He said, "Now I understand. So, that means that you should have a gospel meeting when you need one. Is that right?" I said, "Yes, you are right. We do not do it that way, but that is really the way it should be done."

Two or three months passed, and Wes called me. He said, "We are ready for a gospel meeting, and we would like to start it on Monday night two weeks from now. We have several who are coming, and they are ready to obey the gospel. You come, and they will be present every night." I said, "All right, I will come." The gospel meeting was conducted for three nights—Monday through Wednesday nights. There were baptisms every night. We ended up baptizing eight people into Christ. The ripened grain was ready for harvesting, and the church knew it. Timing is really significant in evangelism. We must be present with the gospel when people are ready to be taught.

My first meeting, that "nine days of grace," speaks

loudly on some important lessons about life in this world and life in the church. Let us remember some of the more significant ones. Little churches can become dear and precious to those who know them. The power of God is resident in the gospel, and it does its work when it is made known. The unity of the church is one of the most beautiful things in the world. We always need each other, and we depend upon each other. It is a wonderful thing for brethren to come together and concentrate on worship, preaching, and praying.

Especially, let us remember that it would be wonderful if all of us could slow down in this hectic world and have time to visit with loved ones in Christ and friends, to worship (even in the open air), and to listen even to the young preach God's Word. If we did so, we would find some beautiful relationships and opportunities that we can find no other way. It seems that we have to slow down in order to catch up; we have to take time out to have time for the important things.

> Take time to be holy,
> Speak oft with thy Lord.
> Abide in Him always,
> And feed on His word;
> Make friends of God's children;
> Help those who are weak;
> Forgetting in nothing
> His blessing to seek.
>
> W. D. Longstaff

☙

*"A missionary is not someone
who has crossed the sea;
he is someone who has seen the cross."*

*"Jesus did not come into the world to preach
the gospel; He came to create it."*

13

THE OBEDIENCE OF FAITH

For you are all sons of God through faith in Christ Jesus (Galatians 3:26).

By faith Abraham, when he was called, obeyed by going out to a place which he was to receive for an inheritance; and he went out, not knowing where he was going (Hebrews 11:8).

When one makes up his mind to be a Christian, he has to come to grips with the meaning of faith; for the Christian life, from start to finish, is a walk of faith. By faith one begins the Christian life, by faith one continues it, and by faith one stays with it until the end. In the words of the apostle Paul, "Salvation is by grace through faith" (Ephesians 2:8, 9).

This truth of the importance of faith raises a dilemma: "Where does one look to find the answer to the fundamental question 'What is faith?'" I learned as I grew in Christ that there is only one place where one can discover this valuable understanding: It is in the Word of God. One cannot look to his friends, his parents, or even the religious world for the answer to this question; only to the Scriptures he must go.

Surprisingly, the basic definition of biblical faith can be written in a single sentence: *Faith is accepting what God has said and acting upon His Word with trust and love.* This simple explanation is succinctly presented to us in one powerful verse of Scripture, Romans 10:17:

> So faith comes from hearing, and hearing by the word of Christ.

The fact affirmed by this verse is that the Scriptures create faith in us, and faith can come in no other way. Hence, true faith presupposes a revelation from God; it assumes that God has spoken and that we have accepted His revelation and are setting out to live by what He has said. Consequently, it is God who builds faith in us, and He does it through the instrument of His divine Word.

The well-known words of Hebrews 11:1 give us a description of what faith does for us:

> Now faith is the assurance of things hoped for, the conviction of things not seen.

Our reason—the very basis—for our expecting God to save us, for our looking to God to answer our prayers, and for our relying on Him to keep all of His other promises to us is what we call faith. The ground of our confidence, the foundation of our assurance in the existence and integrity of God, is our faith.

Appropriately, the Bible does not just define faith, but it also demonstrates it; it not only tells us what faith is, but it also shows us faith working in a life. Any Christian should rejoice and be thrilled over the opportunity to study the man Abraham, for he is the man in the Bible whom God has set forth to be His classic example of genuine faith. Because of his faith, he was called the friend of God (Isaiah 41:8; James 2:23); and, because of his faith, he is said to be the father of the faithful. In other words, all who believe are the children of Abraham, in a sense, because they are living by faith, the same way he lived (Romans 4:16; Galatians 3:7).

Someone has said, "The best way to get an idea across to someone is to wrap it up in a person." God used this wonderful method, and He gave us an object lesson through one of the great men of the Old Testament. He wrapped up in Abraham the truth of what it means to have faith and to live by faith.

Abraham faced three mountain-peak tests in life, and the way he faced these tests illustrates the different elements of faith.

The first component of faith is obeying God's Word.

I know that this statement sounds too simple to be true, but it is undoubtedly the truth. Perhaps its simplicity is the reason many have skipped over it without recognizing the fact of it. Notice how this trait was true of Abraham's faith.

The Lord asked Abraham to depart from Ur of the Chaldeans and Haran, his homes (Genesis 11:27–31), and follow His guidance to another place. His first call, from Ur, is dated around 2165 B.C.; his second one, perhaps as many as fifteen years later, was from Haran. The divine record pictures the second call at Haran in detail,

> Now the Lord said to Abram, "Go forth from your country, and from your relatives and from your father's house, to the land which I will show you; and I will make you a great nation, and I will bless you, and make your name great; and so you shall be a blessing; and I will bless those who bless you, and the one who curses you I will curse. And in you all the families of the earth shall be blessed" (Genesis 12:1–3).

God instructed Abraham to go forth from his country, his kindred, and his father's house. The order catches our attention: Each is progressively stronger, and each is a greater sacrifice. God did not plot out the places to which He was going to take Abraham. He did not give him a forwarding address or supply him with a road map. He just said, "Follow Me, and I will tell you when we get there." Such a command would be a clear test of faith.

After receiving these instructions, what did Abraham do? The text says, "So Abram went forth . . ." (12:4). He was living by faith. He abandoned everything that was really significant to him—country, extended relatives, and immediate kin. Abraham was seventy-five years old when he obeyed God's command (12:4). His faith is beautifully described in Hebrews 11:8:

> By faith Abraham, when he was called, obeyed by going out to a place which he was to receive for an inheritance; and he went out, not knowing where he was going.

Abraham packed his belongings, chopped off his roots, departed from his homeland, and went with the intent of following the Lord to the place He would show him. Because of his going out in this fashion, we call him the Columbus of the faith. When God asked him to leave, he left. God called Abraham's obedience to His command an act of faith.

Analyze this component of his faith.

This element of faith involved listening to God's Word. A command was given, and Abraham heard and understood it. Someone has said, "God is not so much interested in our eyes as He is in our ears." We want to walk by sight, but God wants us to walk by faith. We want to see, but God wants us to believe. The big truth in the

Old and New Testaments is the fact that God says to man, "Will you listen to what I am saying?"

This element of faith involves accepting God's Word. It is one thing to hear what He says and another thing to accept what God says, for God does not always tell us what we want to hear. The message of the Bible is always needed, but it is not always wanted. Joshua was told that he was to encircle Jericho one time each day for six days and then encircle the city seven times on the seventh day. Joshua heard the plan, but did he accept the plan? Yes, by faith he accepted and implemented God's plan, and Jericho fell. Naaman heard that he would have to dip in the Jordan River seven times; but Naaman—at least at first—did not accept it. He did not want that solution to his problem.

Many have heard Jesus say in Mark 16:16, "He who believes and is baptized shall be saved," but they have not accepted it. This issue came up when I was studying the Bible with one of my neighbors when I was in my early twenties. As I pointed out from the Scriptures the way of salvation, he said, "I know that is what that book says, but I do not accept it." His problem was one of the most serious problems a person can have—that of refusing to accept what God has said.

This element of faith involves obeying God's Word. We have finally come around to where we started. Abraham heard God's instructions, he accepted them in his heart, and then he obeyed them. Faith does not run from doing God's Word; faith runs to fulfill it.

Although God has not asked us to depart from our homeland and go out to another place, as He did Abraham, He has asked everyone who would follow Him in faith to lay aside their opinions, personal wishes, and human wisdom, and follow His Word.

Every person has his or her own journey to make from Haran. It may be a journey out of denominationalism into pure New Testament Christianity. It may be a journey out of sinful living into righteous, godly living. It may be a journey out of being one of the crowd into a walk with Christ, even though that walk may have the company of very few human comrades.

The Christian life begins with the Bible; it starts with what the Word says and our decision to live by it. The reason most people do not become Christians is that they do not take the time to get alone with the Bible and find out what God has said so that they can make a truly faith-based decision to be a Christian. I had a professor in a graduate class who liked to say, "After all, every biblical question comes down to 'What does the Bible say?'" Changing his statement just a little, one could say, "After all, every question of faith comes down to 'What does the Bible say?'" You have to go through the written Word to get to and walk with the Living Word, Jesus.

My journey with God began with a simple question: "Will I obey God or not?" When you think about it,

everyone's journey begins with an affirmative answer to
that question. If we are going to walk with God, we have
to walk with Him through obedience to His Word. There
is no other way to walk by faith!

"A little boy said, 'If the Lord were to tell me
to jump through that wall, I would jump—
because I know the Lord would put a hole there.'
Faith does what the Lord commands and trusts
God to work out the circumstances."

"Remember, the order is fact, faith, feeling."

14

TRUSTING IN GOD

In hope against hope he believed, so that he might become a father of many nations, according to that which had been spoken, "So shall your descendants be." Without becoming weak in faith he contemplated his own body, now as good as dead since he was about a hundred years old, and the deadness of Sarah's womb; yet, with respect to the promise of God, he did not waver in unbelief but grew strong in faith, giving glory to God (Romans 4:18–20).

The Christian life—in its commencement, continuation, and consummation—is a life of faith. Paul said, "For we walk by faith, not by sight" (2 Corinthians 5:7). Faith is to a Christian what wings are to a bird. Without wings, a bird cannot fly—and without faith, a Christian cannot be a *Christ*-ian.

God has shown us a picture of faith working in a life in the narratives that are given in Genesis concerning Abraham. As he obeyed God and followed Him to the place that He would show him, he illustrated the first component of faith—notably, that faith obeys God's Word.

The second element of faith is seen in Abraham's response to God's promise that He would give him an heir, a son. It is the characteristic of trusting in God's Word.

When Abram arrived in Canaan, he faced his second gigantic test of faith. God promised Abram that He would bless him. Confused about his future, Abram asked God, "O God, what about the fact that I have no son, no heir?" (Genesis 15:1–6). God said that He had descendants for Abram in His plans, for He was going to give Abram and Sarai a son and through that son He would give Abram a multitude of descendants.

He took him outside and said, "Look up at the heavens and count the stars—if indeed you can count them." Then he said to him, "So shall your descendants be." Abram believed the Lord, and he credited it to him as righteousness (Genesis 15:5, 6).

God also told Abram that he was going to give him Palestine to possess (Genesis 15:7). Abram, wanting assurance, asked Him, "How may I know that I will possess this land?" In response to his question, God engaged in a kind of covenant-making exercise with Abram.

The Old Testament is really the story of God making

covenants with man. God used the current agreement-ritual of Abram's time to express the covenant that He was going to have with Abram. He said to him: "Take a three-year-old heifer, a three-year-old female goat, a three-year-old ram, a turtledove and a young pigeon, and cut the heifer, goat, and ram into two parts." Abram did as he was told, cutting in half the heifer, goat, and ram, and laying each half opposite the other, leaving a path between the halves. He did not cut up the turtledove or the young pigeon. That night a mysterious, flaming pot went down the pathway that was between the pieces (Genesis 15:7–16). That "flaming pot" represented God.

This method of making a covenant probably gave rise to the age-old expression "cutting a covenant." The idea behind it seems to be "If you do not keep this agreement, may you be cut asunder as these animals have been." Typically, both parties would walk between the halves of the carcasses, but in this case God was the One making the covenant. Since this was a one-party covenant, He alone walked down the path.

God went through this routine for Abram's benefit, not for His. God is the eternal God. All of His attributes are perfect; He cannot improve on His perfection. His Word is truth and never contains one particle of error. He does not need to affirm anything with anyone, for He cannot lie. Any promise from Him is as sure as the foundations of the earth, but God went through this ritual so that Abram would have testimony from God for his faith.

Abram's task for the next few years was to trust in God's promises. Evidently, however, Abram and Sarai thought that God was going to give them a son immediately. God did not. After waiting ten years (Genesis 16:3), a period that must have seemed like an eternity to both of them, they decided to do something about it. They chose to take matters into their own hands. Here was a brief breakdown in Abram's faith.

Sarai suggested that Abram take Hagar as a secondary wife to secure a child for them (Genesis 16:1–4). Abram accepted Sarai's suggestion. Since no child had been born to them through Sarai, Abram was likely reasoning that providing an heir through Hagar must be God's way of accomplishing what He had promised. Abram was wrong in what he did, for the promised child was to come through Sarai in God's own time. Abram and Sarai had become too impatient with God.

However, Abram's actions, even though they were wrong and expressed a lack of faith, must be understood against the backdrop of the customs of the day. Though strange to the modern person, the approach Abram and Sarai took to their problem was probably the accepted way of handling this problem in their day and in their culture. The code of Hammurabi[1] and the

---

[1]Hammurabi, a king of Babylon (1728–1686 B.C.), wrote a code of laws for his people that survives to this day. His set of laws drew upon earlier Sumerian legislative materials such as the codes of Eshnunna and Lipit-Ishtar. Several copies of Hammurabi's code were made in the form

Nuzi documents[2] indicate that a barren wife could give a slave to her husband and retain legal rights to the child born to that union. However, after the birth of the child, the slave was to remain in her rightful place of submission as a slave.

A son, Ishmael, was born to Hagar, the handmaiden of Sarai, but God made it clear to Abram that Hagar was not the one through whom the promised posterity would come (Genesis 16:7–16; 17:20, 21). After the birth of Ishmael, Sarai became bitter and wanted Abram to drive Hagar and her son out of the household. The situation caused severe distress for Abram, who did not want to compound the difficulty that already existed. However, to please Sarai, he sent Hagar and her son away.

Abram thought he had already waited a long time for a son, but he had fourteen more years to wait before the son of promise would arrive. Finally, when Abraham was ninety-nine (Genesis 17:1), God spoke to him specifi-

---

of *stelae* and placed in public places so as to bring its contents to the notice of the general public. The social conditions that resulted at the beginning of the second millennium B.C., if not earlier, are clearly indicated by this code.

[2]Excavations of the town of Nuzi to the east of the Tigris has provided archaeologists with an amazing collection of clay documents which have given insight into the customs of the ancient Bible lands. Most of these documents are assigned to the fifteenth century B.C. The customs and laws contained in the tablets show striking parallels to those of the Hebrew Patriarchal society.

cally concerning the coming of Isaac (Genesis 17:15–19; 18:10–15). By this time, however, so many years had passed that both Abram (Genesis 17:17) and Sarai (Genesis 18:12–15) laughed in their hearts about the possibility of having a son. Apparently, their faith had waned.

God gave Abram and Sarai encouragement that He would fulfill His promise to give them a son: He changed their names. Abram was changed to Abraham (Genesis 17:5); and Sarai, to Sarah (Genesis 17:15). The significance of the change was that Abraham was going to become in truth a "father of many nations." Sarah, as the mother of these nations, would be a "princess" before God.

In addition, God formed a covenant with Abraham to confirm that he would give Abraham and Sarah a son. He directed them to circumcise every male of Abraham's household as a "sign of the covenant" God had made with Abraham (Genesis 17:1–14).

> "This is My covenant, which you shall keep, between Me and you and your descendants after you: every male among you shall be circumcised. And you shall be circumcised in the flesh of your foreskin, and it shall be the sign of the covenant between Me and you. And every male among you who is eight days old shall be circumcised throughout your generations, a servant who is born in the house or who is bought with money from any foreigner, who is not of your descendants" (Genesis 17:10–12).

God placed certain covenant obligations upon Abraham even before the son was born. From that time forward, when a male child reached the age of eight days old, he was to be circumcised. The spiritual significance of this circumcision would be that every boy born to the Abrahamic clan was part of the covenant and would have a sign upon him that would indicate this fact.

One reason for inaugurating the sign at this time was that God was preparing Abraham for the birth of Isaac, who would be a tangible fulfillment of the promises of the covenant. He wanted Abraham to be ready to continue the covenant by his putting the sign of the covenant upon the son that would be born to them.

At long last, a son was born to Abraham and Sarah. The son was given the divinely appointed name Isaac, which means "laughter." At his birth, Abraham was one hundred and Sarah was ninety. *Twenty-five years had passed since God had first promised Abraham a son.*

What did God accomplish by allowing the passing of this much time before giving Abraham a son? Why did He wait so long? When you think about it, some good reasons will come to mind. For one thing, this delay constituted a major test of Abraham's faith. Could Abraham believe that God would fulfill His promise after so long a time? His faith did wane to a degree, as we have noticed; but he and Sarah always came back to a state of believing in God's promise.

Further, this delay forced Abraham to realize that the nation that would come forth from him was to be from God alone. God waited until Sarah was past her natural time of bearing children so that He could demonstrate that Abraham's promised descendants would truly be of supernatural origin. Isaac was to be uniquely God's child, though born to Abraham and Sarah. The Bible says,

> Then the Lord took note of Sarah as He had said, and the Lord did for Sarah as He had promised. So Sarah conceived and bore a son to Abraham in his old age, at the appointed time of which God had spoken to him. Abraham called the name of his son who was born to him, whom Sarah bore to him, Isaac. Then Abraham circumcised his son Isaac when he was eight days old, as God had commanded him (Genesis 21:1–4).

We further read in Hebrews 11:11, 12:

> By faith even Sarah herself received ability to conceive, even beyond the proper time of life, since she considered Him faithful who had promised. Therefore there was born even of one man, and him as good as dead at that, as many descendants as the stars of heaven in number, and innumerable as the sand which is by the seashore.

Abraham sagged some in his faith, but he continually

came back to belief. He attempted to take things into his own hands and "help" God keep His promise, but God did not permit it. Abraham clearly demonstrates that true faith must trust in God's promises.

The second action of faith, then, is trusting in God's Word. Any walk of faith will include trust in the Word of God, if it is authentic faith.

Consider carefully this component of faith.

This action of faith involves trusting in God's Word regardless of what you see. Take the command of baptism as an illustration. Have you ever heard someone say of baptism, "I don't see how being immersed in water could have anything to do with salvation"? The truth of the matter is that God does not ask us to see—He asks us to believe! Read Mark 16:15, 16; Acts 2:38; 22:16. He did not ask Abraham to see how He would give him a child—He asked him to believe it!

One of the most obvious places where one is standing on the promises of God is in the water of baptism. The immersion does not wash the body or physically heal the body. It is just a harmless dipping of the body in water. The only thing about baptism that makes it of value is God's promise in connection with it. We do not see any tangible response to a baptism into Christ, such as an audible voice from heaven, a divine spotlight immediately shining around the one coming up out of the water, or some supernatural feeling coming over the one who has been baptized. No visible miracle

occurs. When you are baptized, you are just trusting
in God's promise: You go down into the water trusting,
and you come up out of the water trusting. Baptism is
an act of faith for salvation. When you come up out of
the water, you believe that God in heaven has kept
His Word and washed away your sins in the blood of
Jesus.

*This action of faith involves trusting in God's Word
regardless of your circumstances.* Abraham and Sarah
had grown old, and they had to look to God's word for
their confidence—not to their declining physical bodies.
Everything around them was crying out, "You cannot
have a child. You are too old."

Paul said that Abraham was hoping against hope:

> In hope against hope he believed, so that he might
> become a father of many nations, according to that
> which had been spoken, "So shall your descendants be"
> (Romans 4:18).

Nothing about him—nothing he saw in his body or in
his circumstances—would convince him that he was
going to father a child. It had come down to trusting in
God's promise.

Some people seem to be saying, "I am going to wait
and see what the circumstances say before I make up my
mind." It is as if they are waiting for the circumstances
around them to tell them what God's will is. Circum-

stances cannot tell us God's will; they can only show us the situation in which we will do God's will. God's Word tells us what to do.

This action of faith involves trusting in God's Word regardless of what men may say. When you choose to walk with God, you must understand that you are going to be tied to God through His Word, not through special signs, unusual feelings, the advice of so-called authorities, or mysterious, better-felt-than-told guidance from others. This kind of walk obviously requires daily trust in God through a daily trust in God's Word.

A Christian is a person who makes his or her way through this world trusting in God's Word regardless of what he or she sees, hears, or understands from the secular world. The world laughs and declares that the Christian is "too heavenly minded to be of any earthly good." The Christian responds by saying, "Faith in God is true reality, and this faith enables me to put my circumstances into their proper place in the scheme of things. If I listen to my circumstances and ignore God's Word, I will be a pawn in the hands of whatever may happen. If I trust in God's Word and live for Him regardless of my circumstances, I will be a Christian pilgrim making my way through this world in the power and guidance of God."

God has not chosen to give us any other guidance than His faithful Word. He helps us with His providence, but He does not guide us with it. Our trust in God is based upon our faithful adherence to His Word. Anyone who does not trust in God's Word simply does not trust in God.

*"Faith is not a blind leap into the dark.
It is accepting the evidence that God has given,
obeying His Word, and trusting in God
to keep His promises."*

15

THE SURRENDER OF FAITH

*Isaac spoke to Abraham his father and said,
"My father!" And he said, "Here I am, my son."
And he said, "Behold, the fire and the wood, but
where is the lamb for the burnt offering?" (Genesis
22:7).*

*Then Abraham raised his eyes and looked, and
behold, behind him a ram caught in the thicket by
his horns; and Abraham went and took the ram
and offered him up for a burnt offering in the place
of his son (Genesis 22:13).*

Henry Ford said, "You can do something great if
you break it down into little pieces." Abraham, in his life
with God in the Old Testament, takes the principle of
faith and breaks it down into three component parts: He
says that faith is obeying God's Word, trusting in God's
Word, and surrendering to God's Word.

A few years after the birth of Isaac, Abraham manifested the supreme action of faith, the component of surrendering to God's Word. God asked him to offer Isaac, his son, as a sacrifice to Him, and Abraham obeyed.

The Bible does not tell how old Isaac was at the time Abraham received this command. Perhaps he was not more than ten years of age. He went with his father obediently, even permitting himself to be bound without apparent protest. His question "Where is the lamb for the burnt offering?" (Genesis 22:7) indicates that he was old enough to reason. It also shows that he was young enough not to have asked the question prior to their arrival at the mountain or for his father to have shared this information with him before their departure for the mountain.

When God commanded Abraham to offer Isaac, it almost appears as if He "rubbed in" His command.

> He said, "Take now your son, your only son, whom
> you love, Isaac, and go to the land of Moriah, and offer
> him there as a burnt offering on one of the mountains
> of which I will tell you" (Genesis 22:2).

God did not just say, "Take Isaac." He referred to Isaac in three endearing ways. He said, "Take your son, your only son, whom you love, Isaac."

We are not told what Abraham, deep within his heart, thought about this command. Pagan nations around

Abraham did engage in child sacrifice. It was not done every day, but it was done. Did Abraham think, "God wants me to show Him that I am as dedicated to Him as the pagans around me are to their gods." We do not know how he thought, but we do know that he immediately set out to do what God had commanded him. We see faith at work in a life.

Why did God give such a command as this? From the reading of what happened on Mount Moriah, we know that God did not want a human sacrifice. Therefore, it must be that God wanted Abraham to demonstrate complete trust in Him by giving Him the dearest and most precious possession he had. Remember, God asked for Isaac, not Sarah; for all the promises He had made to Abraham were wrapped up in Isaac, not Sarah. Further, God was not just asking for Abraham's son. He was asking for Abraham's heart and future—He wanted Abraham to place every inch of himself on that altar.

What did Abraham do? After receiving the command, he immediately gathered up the wood and the fire, called together the two servants needed for the journey, and took off on the three-day journey to Mount Moriah, where the sacrifice would be made. When they arrived at the foot of the mountain that God had indicated, Abraham dismissed the servants with the words "I and the lad will go over there; and we will worship and return to you" (Genesis 22:5). Abraham believed confidently in God. He believed that even though he would offer his son on the altar, God would raise him from the dead so that all the promises God had made could be fulfilled through him. The writer of the Book of Hebrews indicated the depth of Abraham's faith in his description of what Abraham did:

> By faith Abraham, when he was tested, offered up Isaac; and he who had received the promises was offering up his only begotten son; it was he to whom it was said, "In Isaac your descendants shall be called." He considered that God is able to raise men even from the dead, from which he also received him back as a type (Hebrews 11:17–19).

On the way up the side of the mountain, Isaac asked a pertinent question. Contemplating what they were going to do, Isaac said, "Father, I have the wood, and you have the knife and the fire, but where is the lamb?" That is a good question, is it not? Isaac must have reasoned, "Why should we go all the way to the top of the mountain if we do not have anything to offer after we get up there?" I imagine that Abraham looked off into the distance or looked up toward the summit of the mountain, bit his lower lip, and with a grimacing face, said, "My son, God will provide."

When Abraham and Isaac reached a level place near the top of the mountain, Abraham must have said, "Right here. This spot is the place." He then silently built the altar that would be used. Piling stone upon stone, he made it sturdy, strong, and appropriate for the sacrifice that was going to be made.

We do not know how Abraham went about the actual offering of Isaac. Perhaps he sat down with Isaac, put his arm around him, and said, "Isaac, you know that I love you with all my heart. All your life I have taught you to believe in God. When God commands, we always obey. Isaac, I am going to have to do something that God has commanded. I do not understand it, but everything will be all right, for God can be trusted. I have taught you to trust in God. We must trust Him completely now. He will take care of both of us if we believe completely in Him. I am going to tie you up and place you upon the altar, but do not be afraid, for God will take care of you. As I place you on the altar, think of God, put your trust in Him, and everything will be all right."

After their man-to-man conversation, Abraham bound Isaac and laid him gently upon the altar. He probably wanted to get it over quickly so that there would be no pain to Isaac. He drew back the knife. It flashed in the sunlight as he prepared to bring it down.

In that split second between his raising the knife and bringing it down, a voice called to him from heaven and said, "Abraham, Abraham! Do not stretch out your hand against the lad, and do nothing to him; for now I know that you fear God, since you have not withheld your son, your only son, from Me" (Genesis 22:11, 12). Abraham had faithfully passed the test of surrendering completely to God's word. He had put on the altar his dearest earthly possession, doing exactly what God had asked him to do without wavering.

The significance of what Abraham did is immediately recognized by anyone who reads the account thoughtfully. We see here the ultimate character of faith—surrender to God's Word.

There comes a time in a person's life when his faith must surrender to God's Word, or else his faith becomes a dead faith. This component of faith will be a trait of everyone's faith, even though it may not be seen in such a dramatic fashion as it was with Abraham's faith. Think about it.

A person of faith surrenders his heart to God's Word. In this sacrifice, Abraham was giving up to God the sacred affections of his heart, the love of his soul, Isaac. Surely, Isaac had been the apple of Abraham's eye, the dream-come-true of his older years. In his sacrificial act, he was trusting God to give Isaac back to him in order that He might fulfill the promises He had made about him.

We actually own only one possession—just one. We cannot claim as our own the land where we live, the houses in which we live, the cars we drive, or the money we might have in the bank. God has given us ownership of only one item—our hearts. God does not look at the appearance; He looks at the heart. In light of this fact, there is only one real gift we can give to God—we can only give Him our hearts. He never asks for anything more of us, for in giving Him our hearts we give Him the proper management of everything He has loaned us. When he gets our hearts, He gets all of us. As Abraham placed Isaac upon the altar, he was giving God the depth of his being, his very heart.

The person who believes will surrender his or her future to God's Word. Why did God ask for Isaac? Why did God not ask for Sarah? Wrapped up in Isaac was Abraham's future. If Abraham did not have an heir, he did not have a future. Beneath the family issue is the future issue. Every promise God had made to Abraham involved Isaac and his descendants. God was saying to Abraham, "I have made you a promise. You know that I will keep it. However, I want you to trust in Me—not in a promise, not in your son, but in your Sovereign Lord. Will you surrender everything in your future to Me by trusting Me?"

The person who believes will surrender his or her dearest treasures to God's Word. What God did with Abraham in this event is illustrated by a fabled story about a man who was converted to God. Shortly after his conversion, God said to him, "What do you have?" He said, "Well, I have a house." God said, "I want it." He said, "All right, it is Yours, Lord." God said, "What else do you have?" He said, "I have a car and some money in the bank." God said, "I want both the car and the money in the bank." He said, "Lord, You are my Lord. If You want my car and my money, they are Yours." God said,

"What else do you have?" He said, "All I have now are my wife and my two children." God said, "I want your wife and your two children." He said, "I surrender my wife and children to You, Lord." God said, "What else do you have?" He said, "I don't have anything now except myself." God said, "I want you too." He said, "All right, Lord, You now have everything and everyone I have. What do You want me to do now?" God said, "I will give all these people and things back to you for you to keep for My glory until I deem it wise to use them in some other way."

Did God not say something similar to Abraham? Did He not say to Abraham, "I want your son, Abraham"? Did Abraham not say, "Lord, here is my son. Now what do You want me to do?" It was then that God said, "I am going to give him back to you until I have further need for him."

The person who believes surrenders everyone and everything to God because he knows that all of these are safe with God. Just think about it. When Abraham gave God his son, God turned around and gave him back to Abraham for time and eternity. God will be no one's debtor. Later, in the New Testament, Jesus spoke of God as being the God of Abraham, Isaac, and Jacob. God *is*, not *was*, Jesus said. All three of them—Abraham, Isaac, and Jacob—were with God in eternity at the time Jesus spoke those words (Matthew 22:32). God gave Isaac back to Abraham forever. Let us remember that our children are safe in the hands of God.

' *The person who believes surrenders all to God because he knows that God will give back to him what he needs to do His will.* Life does not consist in houses, land, money, or even in husbands, wives, or children, as precious as they are. Jesus said that life does not consist of the things that one possesses (Luke 12:15). True life is found in walking with God in faith. Such a walk glorifies and prioritizes all the other relationships we have.

A wealthy man during the Great Depression, I am told, loved to quote Acts 2:38. He would mention it often to show the importance of baptism to others. However, when the collection plate was passed on Sunday morning, he would put in a mere dime. The church was struggling during that time, and even though he had the means to help, he consistently gave only ten cents. He could quote Acts 2:38, but he did not understand it. He did not have the faith it teaches. He had failed to learn that this verse teaches that anyone who truly repents and is baptized begins the walk of faith, a walk that will be characterized by selfless giving and living.

The tests that Abraham passed by faith help us to see what true faith is and how it operates in a person's heart. In particular, we have seen that such a faith can be broken down into three components: obeying God's Word, trusting in God's Word, and surrendering to God's Word.

Have you ever started to walk across a small bridge

but hesitated because you thought it might not hold your weight? You perhaps inched out on it to test its strength—like a boy inching out on an iced-over pond—and finally, you slowly made your way across to the other side. Confident now of its ability to support your weight, you walked back and forth across it with assurance. Perhaps this picture illustrates what it means to live by faith. You accept the evidence of God's Word, and you place all your weight on that truth from God. You stand upon that truth, live upon that truth, and go into eternity relying upon that truth. Your bridge to God is the truth of His Word. The walk of faith is not based upon feelings, suppositions, or supposed signs. It is a walk right down the middle of the bridge of God's Word.

You may ask, "Are there any rewards to such a walk?" Two significant rewards are mentioned in the Scriptures. The faithful person not only gets the blessings of God, but he or she also gets God. God is not only our Redeemer, but also our reward. The greatest gift from God is God. In Genesis 15:1 God had said to Abraham:

> Do not fear, Abram, I am a shield to you; your reward shall be very great.

As Abraham walked with God, he not only got God's blessings, but he also got the Blesser.

The same invitation is offered to each of us. God says, "Come walk with Me, and I will give you My presence and My provisions." The good news from God is that the walk of faith opens the door to all that God offers. Faith is not only the way *of* life, but it also is the way *to* life!

∾

"Man says, 'Seeing is believing,'
but the Bible says, 'Believing is seeing.'"

"Only what we give to God do we get to keep."

16

THE GOD OF ALL TOMORROWS

Jesus Christ is the same yesterday and today and forever (Hebrews 13:8).

But do not let this one fact escape your notice, beloved, that with the Lord one day is like a thousand years, and a thousand years like one day (2 Peter 3:8).

Are we not glad that God has placed a veil over the future so that we cannot see it? If He allowed us to view the tomorrows that may be ahead of us, we undoubtedly would not be able to handle that kind of knowledge. We would be like the dog chasing a car down a country road. Suppose he caught the car? What would he do with a car? In the same vein, what would a human being do with intimate knowledge of the future?

Saul thought that he wanted to see the events of the

next day (1 Samuel 28:6, 7). He had gone to the Lord about it, but the Lord had not answered him. In desperation, he found a medium and asked her to bring up Samuel, the renowned prophet, from the dead. For a reason that is not revealed to us, God miraculously allowed Samuel, who had died a few months before, to come up for a few minutes from the other world. The medium was as surprised as anyone, for she had never brought up a departed spirit. Saul was granted permission to ask Samuel the question "What about tomorrow?" Samuel told him that he would die on the field of battle the next day.

Hearing Samuel's answer, Saul fell over like a dead man. A picture of the future would knock over any man! It took everyone present, using all the resources at their command, even to get Saul to stand up and receive nourishment. If we were given a divine glimpse of the misty future, it would no doubt overwhelm us. God has graciously shielded us from the unknown days and events that are perhaps coming. God will handle what is coming; in His kindness and care for us, He has asked us to deal only with the present.

Someone has wisely said, "We do not know what the future holds, but we do know who holds the future." The good news about tomorrow is that God is in it, He is over it, and He is controlling it. Do not tremble before the future; do the only thing you can do about it: Trust God regarding it. The true sentiment of all of us is surely reflected by the words of an unknown poet:

So, I go on not knowing—
   I would not know if I might;
I would rather walk in the dark with God
   than go alone in the light;
I would rather walk with Him by faith
   than walk alone by sight.

All of this thinking about the future raises the question "What kind of God will our heavenly Father be to us tomorrow?" Let us look at what He has been. Then, on the basis of His constancy, we can project that picture into the future. In other words, what He was yesterday, He will be tomorrow.

We know that He will be a God of grace tomorrow. He has always answered us with grace and not with judgment. His initial response has always been with lovingkindness. Through what we have seen in the past, we can know that, when we make a mistake or sin, God will offer His forgiveness to us. He will want to correct our sin and cleanse it. Before judgment, He will always extend mercy. He is a God of power, but His power will be under the control of His love.

Ancient Israel had spurned the love of God again and again. They had gone into sin and idolatry. How did God appeal to them and seek to win them back to faithfulness? He held up His grace.

   "Come now, and let us reason together," says the
Lord, "though your sins are as scarlet, they will be as

white as snow; though they are red like crimson, they will be like wool. If you consent and obey, you will eat the best of the land; but if you refuse and rebel, you will be devoured by the sword." Truly, the mouth of the Lord has spoken (Isaiah 1:18–20).

A time of judgment would come if they did not repent, but God's first offer to them was His cleansing and restoration. Are we not glad that this is the kind of God He will be tomorrow?

Further, we know that He will be a God of truth tomorrow. God will always be on the side of the truth, for He is truth. All authentic truth emanates from Him, and He cannot deny Himself.

One of the sad stories of the Old Testament is the one of the unnamed prophet who was commissioned by the Lord to deliver a rebuke to Jeroboam at Bethel (1 Kings 13:1–3). He was told to give the message to the king and then leave. He was not to stop, to eat, or to visit with anyone. The command was clear and specific. He knew what to do and how to do it. He could have gone down in history as one of the greatest prophets of the Old Testament for walking before the powerful potentate Jeroboam and telling him that he was leading Israel into sin. However, one of the main things that we remember about him is that he backslid in his own Bible study. We remember his disobedience, not his obedience.

When invited, he went home with an older prophet who had "lied" to him. He was punished for listening to a man—even another prophet—instead of listening to God. His lifeless body was found later along the side of the road, having been mauled by a lion. The words on his grave marker could well have been "Here lies a courageous but disobedient prophet."

No one can read through the Bible without being impressed with the truth that God requires obedience. He does not demand perfection, but He expects faithfulness.

As you hold a Bible in your hand, you can say, "Here is the spiritual truth that God chose to reveal to us." We know, of course, that there is far more spiritual truth than what God has given us in the Scriptures, like truth about the origin of the devil and angels; but in the Scriptures God has placed before us the body of spiritual truth that He expects us to follow. He has always taught His people to honor and reverence His Word, and we can know that He will be this same God in the future.

In addition, tomorrow He will be a God who desires our fellowship. One of the remarkable truths that we have seen in the Bible is the truth that God seeks our company. At the dawn of time, God came walking in the cool of the afternoon, anticipating fellowship with His family, Adam and Eve (Cenesis 3).

Every year I have taught at Harding, I have been asked by at least one student, "Why did God make man? After all, He knew that he was going to sin and break His heart, so why did He make the race of men?" There is an answer to this question that we must not run past. That answer can be given by asking another question: "Why does a couple want to have children?" We all know the answer to that question: They want to have a family whom they can love and who will one day love them in return. If you were to ask me, "What is God like?" I would point a finger at you and say, "He is like you!" He is not like your body, but He is like the real you—your spirit, your heart, your mind. He thinks, believes, loves, converses, and enjoys fellowship. If God is like us and we are like God—if we are the offspring of God—why are we surprised that God wanted to have a family even as all of us do?

The Bible is the story of God's family, the human race. Of course, the story is on a far higher level than the story of our physical families, but the heart of that story is that God seeks man's love and companionship. When Adam sinned, God asked him, "Adam, where are you?" God took the initiative and came looking for him. He sought Adam before Adam thought about seeking Him.

Martin Luther said that our prayers to God are like a baby's talk to his parents. A baby can say only a few simple words that are superficial and disconnected. However, the parents enjoy them. Fathers rush home from a busy day to hear them; mothers tuck them away in their memory banks to cherish for years to come.

In a similar way, our prayers are weak, deficient, and

lacking in depth. We may think that God could not possibly be interested in what we are saying to Him. When these thoughts come to us, we just need to remember that God has a tender love toward us that is similar to the love a mother has for her child. God is eager to listen to His children even though we stammer, stutter, and have only a vague understanding of what we are talking about with Him.

> Just as a father has compassion on his children,
> So the Lord has compassion on those who fear Him
> (Psalm 103:13).

God has always wanted our fellowship, and He will be the same God tomorrow. He will love us, and He will yearn for us to love Him in return.

Tomorrow, God will be a God who is approached through Jesus. Someone has said, "The story of the Old Testament is the story of a nation; but the story of the New Testament is the story of a Person." In other words, the Old Testament forms the background for the bringing of the Messiah into the world; then, the New Testament is the revelation of the Messiah's coming and the history of the church He set up.

Christianity is a God-centered religion. Jesus' own affirmation was that He is the only way to God.

> "I am the way, and the truth, and the life; no one comes to the Father, but through Me" (John 14:6).

God has given the Christ preeminence over all powers and rulers because of His suffering for our salvation.

> Being found in appearance as a man, He humbled Himself by becoming obedient to the point of death, even death on a cross. For this reason also, God highly exalted Him, and bestowed on Him the name which is above every name, so that at the name of Jesus every knee will bow, of those who are in heaven and on earth and under the earth, and that every tongue will confess that Jesus Christ is Lord, to the glory of God the Father (Philippians 2:8–11).

Jesus was given as head over all things, including the church; and He will remain as head of this kingdom/church until the end of time. Then He will return the kingdom/church to the Father (1 Corinthians 15:24). There has been, there is, and there will be no other mediator between God and us except Jesus Christ:

> For there is one God, and one mediator also between God and men, the man Christ Jesus (1 Timothy 2:5).

Many of us resolved a long time ago that our lives would be *Christ*-ian lives, and that resolve must be our commitment for the future. We have come to the Lord Jesus through the inspired, written Word; and

Jesus will bring us to the True and Living Father daily and at the end of the way.

> Whether you go,
>> or whether you stay,
> Hold on to Jesus,
>> He knows the way.

We must remember, however, that tomorrow He will be a God of judgment. He is our Savior now, but He will be our Judge then. He is a righteous God and cannot ignore sin. No one can look at the cross and not be constrained to draw this conclusion.

At times in history God has shown His judgment of sin in vivid and horrible ways. He has done this for our learning and understanding (Romans 15:4). Think of the great flood of Genesis 6, the destruction of Sodom and Gomorrah (Genesis 19:23), and the extermination of Canaanites in Palestine (Joshua 6). In these awful cases of judgment, God declared for all to see that He will step in, at the end of time, and make an eternal announcement of His disdain for sin through His final judgment.

Because of who God is, let us not worry about the future. Do not fret over tomorrow or be fearful of it. Let Jesus cheer you with His statement "Be of good cheer, I have overcome the world." When we reach the future, we will find that God has already been there and has gotten it ready for us. He is now going before us and preparing the way by smoothing over the hills and building up the valleys for His children. He went before His people in the Old Testament and drove out all the enemies who would have harmed them. He will also go before His people of the Christian Age and deal with any troubles that may arise. It is the Christian and "the sword of the Lord" facing every tomorrow. We do not even have to be afraid of biological death, for Jesus said:

> I am the resurrection and the life; he who believes in Me will live even if he dies, and everyone who lives and believes in Me will never die . . . (John 11:25, 26).

God sits over time and sees it from its past, present, and future. He sees the end from the beginning. He lives in the eternal now, for He is the Great I Am, the eternally existent One. He is constantly working to bring us from time into eternity, to enjoy His eternal presence forever.

As we look back over the way we have come, therefore, we see how God has led us, loved us, and lavished His blessings upon us. He has been our hope and stay in all the ages past. No, He will not fail us tomorrow. What He has been, He will be. We can hug to our hearts the glorious truth that God changes not. As James said, with God "there is no variation or shifting shadow" (James 1:17).

A father and his little son were crossing a busy street. The traffic was heavy, and they had to watch carefully as they dashed to the other side. At a break in the traffic, the father took the little boy by the hand, and they rushed across the street. When they were safely on the other side, the little tyke said, "Daddy, I was really holding on!" as if it all had depended on him. The father said, "Yes, son, and I was holding on to you." What the little fellow did not realize was that his father had a tighter grip on his little son than his little son had on him. The big hand of the father provided the safety of the boy. It is true that we must hold on to God, but let us also remember that He will be holding on to us and that His grip on us will be much stronger than our grip on Him. He will see us through the busy streets of life and land us safely before His throne of love, peace, and redemption. When we arrive before His throne, we will enter into the eternal life for which we have been preparing through the years.

> So long Thy pow'r has blest me,
> Sure it still will lead me on
> O'er moor and fen, o'er crag and torrent,
> Till the night is gone,
> And with the morn those angel-faces smile,
> Which I have loved long since,
> And lost a while.
>
> J. B. Dykes

ᔕᔑᕉ

*"God has not promised us smooth sailing,
but He has promised us a happy landing."*

*"Do not focus on your problems;
focus on His power and promises."*

*"Life can only be understood backwards,
but it must be lived forwards."*
—*Sören Kierkegaard*